A Discovery Learning Programme for Primary History

Unlocking History

5th Class

FOLENS

First published in 2013 by: Folens Publishers,

Hibernian Industrial Estate, Greenhills Road,

Tallaght, Dublin 24.

Educational Consultants: Simon and Rozz Lewis

Acknowledgements: Extract taken from Tom Barry Guerrilla Years in Ireland, reprinted by kind permission from Mercier Press Ltd., Cork. Alamy, Getty Images, iStockphoto, Thinkstock, Shutterstock, Library of Congress, National Library of Ireland – Image of 'Christain Brothers School, Youghal, Co. Cork', 'Boys from De La Salle Classroom', 'Workhouse in Ballinrobe: From Road to Lough Mask', courtesy of the National Library of Ireland. Wikimedia Commons – image 'Domed Temple Memorial Gardens, Dublin' by Osioni at en.wikimedia [Public Domain] from http://commons.wikimedia.org/wiki/File:Domed_Temple,_Memorial_Gardens,_Dublin.jpg?uselang=en-gb. Image 'Time for Peace' by Miossec at en.wikimedia [Public Domain] from http://upload.wikimedia.org/wikipedia/commons/5/55/Time_for_Peace.jpg. Image 'Mary Robinson, Barack Obama 2009' by Hekerui at en.wikimedia [Public Domain] from http://commons.wikimedia.org/wiki/File:Mary_Robinson,_Barack_Obama_2009.jpg?uselang=en-gb. Image of 'Eleanor Roosevelt Portrait, 1933' by MartinHagberg at en.wikimedia [Public Domain] from http://upload.wikimedia.org/wikipedia/commons/2/22/Eleanor_Roosevelt_portrait_1933.jpg. Image of 'Kevin Barry' by Keogh Brothers Ltd. at en.wikimedia [Public Domain] from http://upload.wikimedia.org/wikipedia/commons/d/d8/Kevin_Barry.jpg. Image of 'St Brendan Celebrating Mass' by HTO at en.wikimedia [Public Domain] from http://commons.wikimedia.org/wiki/File:St._Brendan_celebrating_a_mass.jpg?uselang=en-gb. Image 'Irish Famine Memorial Philadelphia' by Alexmar983 at en.wikimedia [Public Domain] from http://commons.wikimedia.org/wiki/File:Irish_famine_memorial_philadelphia_01.jpg. Image of 'Kevin Barry Ratvilly, Co Carlow' by The Banner at en.wikimedia [Public Domain] from http://commons.wikimedia.org/wiki/File:Kevinbarryrathvilly2.jpg?uselang=en-gb. Image 'Rokotov Portrait Catherine II' by Ф. С. Рокотов at en.wikimedia [Public Domain] from http://commons.wikimedia.org/wiki/File:Rokotov_Portrait_Catherine_II.jpg?uselang=en-gb. Image 'Angela Merkel' by Denniss at en.wikimedia [Public Domain] from http://commons.wikimedia.org/wiki/File:Angela_Merkel_(2008).jpg. Image 'Eleanor Roosevelt and the United Nations Declaration of Independence' by US National Archives Bot at en.wikimedia [Public Domain] from http://commons.wikimedia.org/wiki/File:Eleanor_Roosevelt_and_United_Nations_Universal_Declaration_of_Human_Rights_in_Spanish_text_-_NARA_-_195981.tif. Image 'Mary Robinson in Somalia' by Trocaire at en.wikimedia [Public Domain] from http://commons.wikimedia.org/wiki/File:Mary_Robinson_in_Somalia.jpg?uselang=en-gb. Image' Kevin Barry Commemorative Plaque' by The Banner at en.wikimedia [Public Domain] from http://commons.wikimedia.org/wiki/File:Kevin_Barry_Commemorative_Plaque.jpg?uselang=en-gb. Image ' Mia Nefertiti' by Angelo Atzei at en. Wikimedia [Public Domain] fromhttp://commons.wikimedia.org/wiki/File:Mia_nefertiti.jpg?uselang=en-gb.

ISBN: 978-1-78090-100-8

Contents

Introduction

'**Unlocking History**' is a complete history programme for teachers, parents and pupils. It covers the history curriculum from 3rd to 6th Class and has been developed by primary school teachers. For each class a separate textbook, teacher's manual and exclusive digital resources are integrated to create a unique learning experience.

The programme has three main objectives:

1. The creation of a seamless and blended approach to the teaching and learning of history using historical evidence, active learning, collaborative learning and the incorporation of digital resources that have been specifically designed to complement the programme.

2. The development of key components of the history curriculum: local studies; early people and ancient societies; life, society, politics, conflict, work and culture in the past; national and international history.

3. The establishment of a history series that focuses on the key skills of a historian:
   - empathy
   - time and chronology
   - using historical evidence
   - cause and effect
   - change and continuity
   - synthesis and communication

Chapter Opener

Each chapter opens with a motivating 'hook'. This can be used as an introduction to the topic and lesson. Pupils are drawn into each new topic using a range of stimuli that set the tone for the lesson to follow.

Think and Discuss

Pupils are asked to think about and discuss what they can see in the chapter; in doing so, previous related knowledge is recalled. This provides an opportunity for the development of oral language skills as well as focusing on historical skills.

What Will I Learn?

The curriculum objectives are vitally important for the teacher to plan their lesson. From the curriculum objectives, the pupils are given clear, easy-to-follow learning objectives at the start of every chapter.

Key Vocabulary

Any new vocabulary that is being introduced is presented here. There are many activities that can stem from this. The teacher may need to ensure that all key vocabulary is understood before the lesson development. The key vocabulary is also highlighted throughout each chapter and explained in the glossary section.

The Key to Literacy

The Key to Literacy is an effective tool used to integrate the English curriculum into the history curriculum in a meaningful way that supports the aims of the history curriculum.

Checkpoint

These activities are designed to help facilitate the recall of any historical knowledge that has been learned. Checkpoints link in with the chapter's learning outcomes and are a useful revision tool.

Research and Write It/Over to You/Design and Draw

Each of these sections provide ideas for further extension work in the particular area of historical discovery. This may involve research using the Internet, books or real-life research.

Date It/History Detective

There is a strong emphasis throughout the programme on sequencing past events through the use of timelines. Many attractive and engaging timelines are included throughout. Date It activities also provide opportunities for the child to practise this important skill.

Lesson Wrap-Up/Visual Summary

This component of the chapter provides a quick revision of the chapter's main ideas and themes. This also signals the third and final part of the lesson to the teacher.

Review

The Review focuses on recalling information and vocabulary, critical thinking and developing the skills of a historian.

What Did I Learn? – Self-Assessment

This section provides an important opportunity to reflect upon the lesson. The following questions are asked at the end of every chapter:

- What have I learned in this chapter?
- What else would I like to know?
- Where can I find this information?

Questions can be linked back to learning outcomes and also enable the teacher to assess information and skills that have been learned, provoking further research into areas the pupils are interested in.

Glossary

This is a useful aid as all the words in the Key Vocabulary section are fully explained here in simple, clear and concise language.

Timeline

The Timeline provides a visual overview of the historical periods covered in the series. While all key dates are included, those dates that relate specifically to the topics covered in the child's own book are differentiated in the timeline using a bold black outline. In this way, it becomes very clear to the child how the topics they have learned fit in to the overall context of time.

Chapters – Strands – Strand Units

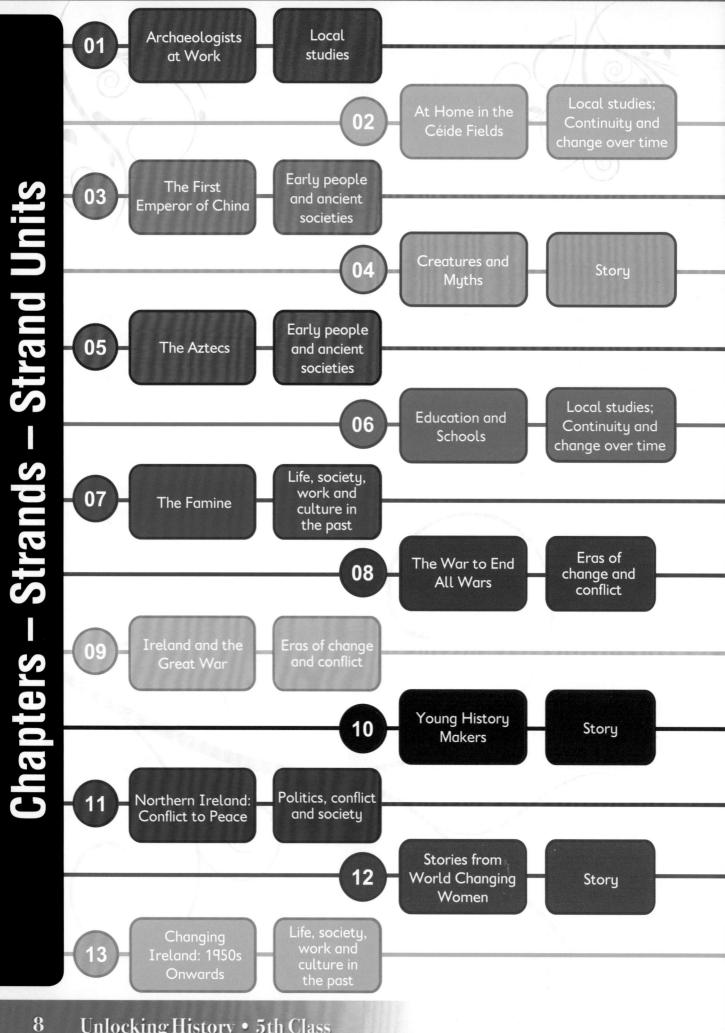

01	Archaeologists at Work	Local studies
02	At Home in the Céide Fields	Local studies; Continuity and change over time
03	The First Emperor of China	Early people and ancient societies
04	Creatures and Myths	Story
05	The Aztecs	Early people and ancient societies
06	Education and Schools	Local studies; Continuity and change over time
07	The Famine	Life, society, work and culture in the past
08	The War to End All Wars	Eras of change and conflict
09	Ireland and the Great War	Eras of change and conflict
10	Young History Makers	Story
11	Northern Ireland: Conflict to Peace	Politics, conflict and society
12	Stories from World Changing Women	Story
13	Changing Ireland: 1950s Onwards	Life, society, work and culture in the past

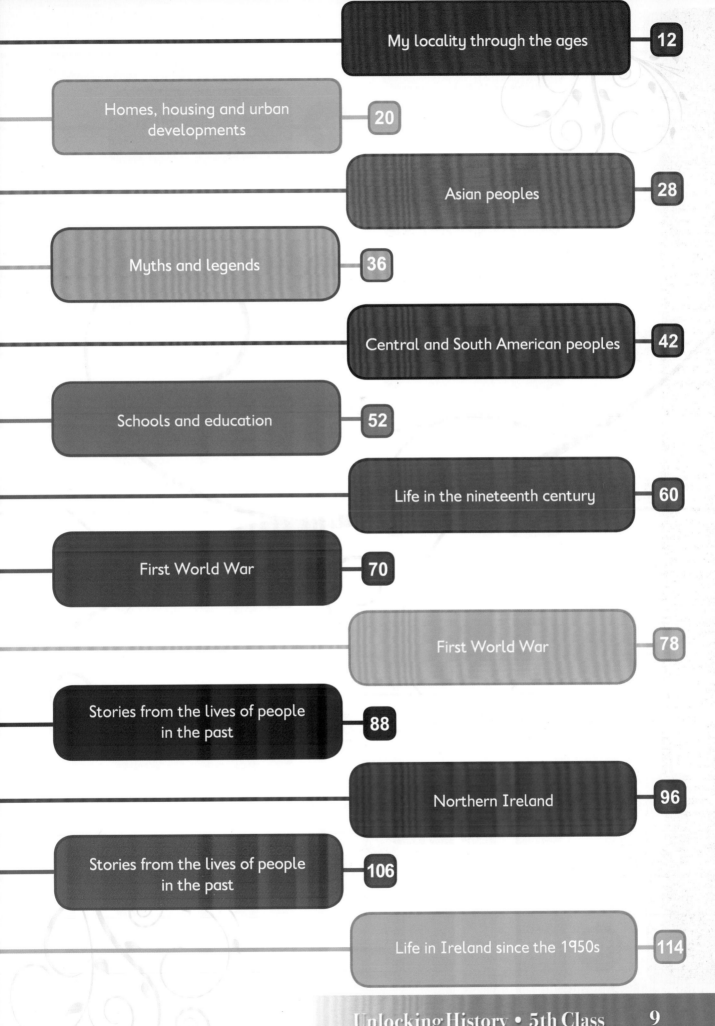

Linkage and Integration

Geography – map the local area

Music – listen to music about events that happened in the locality

English – read local myths and legends

12

Geography – the study of bogs

English – write stories from the perspective of people in the past

Science – explore elements

20

Visual arts – make clay models

Geography – the geography of China

Drama – explore the strict rule of the Qin dynasty through drama

28

Geography – study myths and legends from different countries

Visual arts – design and construct mythical creatures

SPHE – understand peoples feelings and emotions

36

Drama – role play an Aztec event

Visual arts – look at and respond to Aztec art

Geography – study facts about Mexico

42

Gaeilge – an scoil

Visual arts – explore the painting 'The Village School 1665' by Jan Steen

English – read poems about school, such as 'Please Mrs. Butler' by Allan Ahlberg

52

Science – analysis of food and nutrition

Music – listen to traditional music about the Famine, e.g. 'The Fields of Athenry'

Drama – role play scenes such as an eviction or farewell at a harbour

60

Geography – learn about the countries involved in the war

English – read war poetry

Visual arts – look at and respond to depictions of the war

70

Geography – mark places where Irishmen fought on a world map

PE – learn Irish dancing steps

78

English - read stories and poems about the characters mentioned in the chapter

Visual arts - draw/make a death mask like the one worn by Tutankhamun

88

English – write a newspaper article about a major event in Northern Ireland's history

Geography – identify other regions of conflict on a world map

96

Science – explore the contributions of female scientists

English – read poetry by great female poets

Visual arts – depict these women in interesting ways

106

Maths – collect and display data on changes in population over time

English – read poems and stories about emigration

114

1 Archaeologists at Work

What Will I Learn?

- About the study of ancient objects, known as archaeology.
- How an archaeologist works.
- To investigate a historical site and write a field trip report.

Think and Discuss

1. Describe what you see in each photo.

2. What tools can you see being used? What are they being used for?

3. What is the man with the hat holding?

4. How do you think you would feel if you uncovered an ancient skeleton?

5. Do you think there are any dangers in using a powerful digger at a historical site?

6. There are some pieces of historical evidence in the photos. Do you think they are primary or secondary sources?

Key Vocabulary

archaeologist   fieldwork

magnetometer

excavate   periscope

Egyptologist   Romanesque

An Archaeologist

Hi, my name is Emer and I am an archaeologist. I study the remains left behind by people who lived in the past. The first part of my job involves finding and recording evidence of people living in the past. This is called fieldwork.

Some sites, such as churches and deserted villages, are easy to find. Other sites cannot be seen on the surface. I use photographs of the ground taken from aircraft or satellites to hunt them down. I look for bumps in the ground where there may have been buildings or walls.

At the site, I use a device called a magnetometer to identify archaeological sites below ground. It is helpful to know if there is something down there before we start digging. Sometimes I use a periscope. This is like a long tube with a camera at the end. It allows me to look through a small opening into an underground tomb.

When we think we have found a good site it is time to excavate. We remove the top layer of soil first. Then we create a grid of squares using rope. Each square is carefully dug up – that is why a site is often called a 'dig'.

The team works very slowly, using a trowel, spoons and brushes to gently scrape away soil. Once an object is dug up, it is given a label and number. We also map the whole area of the site, to show where everything was found. Sometimes I spray on a special chemical to stop an object rotting. I also take very careful notes about the area around the site.

After the digging is over, I examine all the objects that have been found. I try to work out how old a site is, which groups of people lived there, and how they lived. It is like putting together the pieces of a jigsaw.

Did You Know?

In Ireland, all archaeological objects found that have no known owner become the property of the state. All findings must be reported to the Gardaí or the National Museum.

Checkpoint

1. What does an archaeologist do?

2. What devices do archaeologists use to find sites?

3. Name three objects that are used to remove the soil at a dig.

Think About It

1. Why do you think some sites cannot be seen on the surface of the ground?

2. How does a periscope help an archaeologist?

3. Why is the site divided into squares?

4. Why does an archaeological team need to dig very slowly and carefully, do you think?

5. Why do you think an archaeologist makes careful notes about the area around a site?

6. Why do you think some digs are deeper than others?

Research and Write It

The pictures here show Trim Castle in County Meath and the ancient tomb at Knowth, also in County Meath. Using the internet or library books, find out more about these two historical sites. Then compare and contrast them. How old are they? When were they excavated? What artefacts were found during the excavations? Write your findings in a report.

▲ Trim Castle

 Passage tomb at Knowth, County Meath

The Study of Ancient Things

The word archaeology means 'the study of ancient things'. Archaeologists find, dig up and study ancient remains. Some remains lie on the surface. Most of the time, however, they are buried in the soil. So the job of an archaeologist often combines the thrill of treasure hunting with the skills of a detective.

Archaeologists dig up objects made or used by people, such as buildings, tools, weapons, pottery, jewellery and art. These objects are called artefacts. Archaeologists also look for remains of living things. These include the bones of animals that were eaten, seeds from plants that were grown or gathered for food, and the burnt wood from ancient fires.

There are many types of archaeology. Some archaeologists study ancient human beings who lived before history was written down. An Egyptologist studies ancient Egypt, while Classical archaeologists examine ruins from ancient Greek and Roman times.

A 'site' is a place archaeologists want to explore. Some sites are discovered by accident, by farmers or builders, while working at their jobs. Some sites are underwater. The archaeologists working here use the same methods as on land, but they are also trained as divers. They explore the wrecks of sunken ships as well as underwater ruins.

Archaeologists often work in teams. The diggers, or excavators, are often students training to be professional archaeologists. Photographers and artists make a visual record of the site and the objects found. Other members of the team record and label the artefacts. Scientists also test them in a laboratory. Some are experts on plants and animals. Then all the evidence is put together to build up a picture of how people lived in the past.

Think About It

1. Why is an archaeologist like a detective?

2. How do farmers and builders often find artefacts and sites by accident, do you think?

3. What do you think scientists test the artefacts for?

Hi I'm Billy. I am nine years old and I want to be a famous archaeologist when I grow up. I'm going to tell you all about our history field trip. Our school is in Bandon, County Cork, so we decided to visit two historic sites located in Munster. Before we went, we looked at a map of Munster, along with some books on the history of the region.

Our first visit was to the stone circle at Castlenalact, near to Bandon. There are four big stones standing in a row. They are known as megaliths, or 'great stones'. Our teacher said they may be over 3,000 years old. I never knew that people were living in my area so long ago! No one knows exactly why the stones are there. Perhaps an important person is buried nearby.

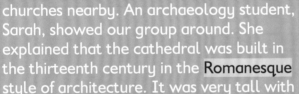

Our next stop was a trip to Ardfert in County Kerry. The monastery here was founded by a famous saint, St Brendan the Navigator. In legend, St Brendan sailed a small leather boat all the way across the Atlantic to America in the sixth century AD. On the way, he met a terrifying sea monster! Our teacher showed us a picture that was drawn in a book hundreds of years later.

At Ardfert, we split into groups to look at the cathedral and the two churches nearby. An archaeology student, Sarah, showed our group around. She explained that the cathedral was built in the thirteenth century in the Romanesque style of architecture. It was very tall with thick walls. One of the churches, Temple-na-Griffin, was named after the monsters carved in stone on one wall. They had heads like dragons and spiked tails. Then came the best part of the trip: we got to look at the archaeologists working on a dig in the cathedral. They were using trowels and brushes to excavate the soil. They didn't find any new artefacts while we were watching, but Sarah showed us the skeleton of a monk along with some objects buried alongside him. It was a bit spooky! Later, at the visitor centre, Sarah showed us one of the coins found at the site. Imagine all the different people who held it hundreds of years ago!

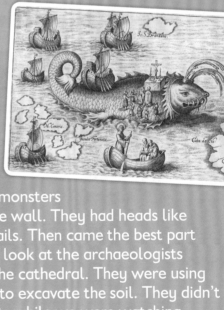

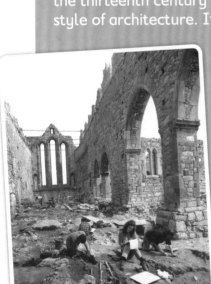

Think and Discuss

1. What sources of evidence did Billy's class use to learn about the history of Munster? State whether each source is a primary or secondary source.

2. Do you think it would have been possible for St Brendan to sail to America all those centuries ago? Give reasons for your answer.

3. Why do you think burials can tell us a lot about how people lived?

4. Describe this coin found at Ardfert Cathedral. How can coins tell us about the past, do you think?

Design and Draw

Imagine you are an archaeologist working on site. It is your job to draw artefacts as they are dug up. Draw the gargoyle pictured here, which was found at Ardfert Cathedral and dates from the fifteenth century. Try to be as accurate as you can. Can you think of an advantage of drawing an artefact over photographing it?

Over to You

Listen to the ballad *Saint Brendan's Fair Isle*, written about the voyage of St Brendan. The song talks about dragons and monsters that swallow sailing ships, demons that burn sailors alive, and St Brendan walking on the waves. What do the words tell you about this voyage across the Atlantic? How reliable are they as historical evidence?

The Key to Literacy

Imagine you are an archaeologist looking for volunteers to help out at a dig over the summer holidays. Write an advertisement for the job. What skills and qualities do you think your volunteers will need? To get people interested, highlight the good things about working on a dig.

Lesson Wrap-Up

Visual Summary

Archaeologists find, dig up and study ancient remains. These remains help us to understand how people in the past lived.

There are many different types of archaeologists. Some work underwater, others specialise in a certain period of history. For example, Egyptologists study ancient Egypt.

Archaeologists work in teams. Some members carry out the digging work, while others record the objects found. Scientists carry out tests to see how old the objects are or what they are made of.

What Did I Learn?

What have I learned in this chapter?

What else would I like to know?

Where can I find this information?

Review

1. Recall
What do archaeologists use a periscope for?

2. Vocabulary
I begin with the 4th letter of the alphabet. I am another word for an archaeological site. I rhyme with 'big'. What am I?

3. Critical Thinking
Compare an underground archaeological site to one located underwater. How are they different and how are they the same? Would archaeologists use the same methods on both? Why?/Why not?

4. Be a Historian!
Organise a class field trip to examine a historic site in your area. Plan your field trip. Decide what you will need to bring with you, what to do when you are there and what you will do when you get back to the classroom. Can you get a local expert to give you a tour? When you visit the site, record your findings in a field trip log.

2 At Home in the Céide Fields

What Will I Learn?

- About the discovery of a Stone Age house at the Céide Fields in North Mayo.
- About the history of another house in the same area.
- How we can use sources of evidence to study the houses in our own local areas.

The Discovery of the Céide Fields

The Stone Age site at the Céide Fields in County Mayo was first discovered in the 1930s. A local schoolteacher, named Patrick Caulfield, noticed that there were piles of stones under the peat bog as he cut his turf. He saw that the stones were not piled in a natural way. Humans must have put them there, he thought. Also, he noticed that they were under the peat bog, which meant they were very ancient.

Years later his son Seamus became an archaeologist and began to study the field walls. He found that the Céide Fields is a huge Stone Age landscape, over 5,000 years old. Apart from the field walls it also contains the remains of Stone Age tombs and houses. We know that after a few hundred years of use, the fields were abandoned, possibly because of climate change. In 1993 a visitor centre was built to explain this landscape to people. It was built to look like a pyramid rising out of the bog.

Think and Discuss

1. Find the pyramid-shaped visitor centre in the photographs. Do you think it is important to have a visitor centre? Why?/Why not?

2. What do the wooden posts inside the visitor centre represent, do you think?

3. What are the people doing in the photograph?

4. Can you see any modern houses in the aerial photograph? What would it be like to live in this place today, do you think?

5. What do you think it was like to live in this place during the Stone Age?

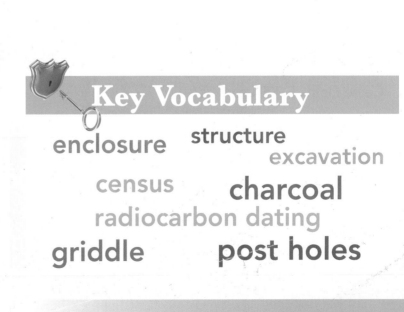

Key Vocabulary

enclosure structure

excavation

census charcoal

radiocarbon dating

griddle post holes

Uncovering the Stone Age

If you go to the Céide Fields visitor centre today you will be taken on a guided tour outside to look at the site. Apart from the field walls, and a Stone Age court tomb, one of the things that you will be shown is the site of a Stone Age house.

It is located near the visitor centre building. It is one of several house sites discovered at the Céide Fields. These houses would have been wooden

▲ Ruins of Stone Age House

structures with thatched roofs. It is very likely that many more house sites lie undiscovered beneath the peat bog. This house site near the visitor centre has been excavated by archaeologists. The site is located in the townland of Glenulra.

The first excavations at Glenulra took place between 1970 and 1972. By that time, much of the bog had been cut away by local people for use as turf. This is how the house site was first discovered. A clue was that the stone walls did not run in a straight line like other walls at the Céide Fields. The first job the archaeologists had to do was to survey and map the house site, using tape measures and other measuring instruments. This is done to mark the exact location of all of the features of the house, as well as any Stone Age artefacts found. Archaeologists also recorded the site using photographs, including aerial photos of the site taken from a plane. They also wrote about their findings in notebooks.

Digging and scraping carefully, using hand trowels, helped archaeologists to find evidence from the site. Any artefacts found were numbered and put into storage boxes to be further studied at a university. The results of this excavation tell us many things about the Stone Age farmers who lived in the area of the Céide Fields 5,000 years ago.

Did You Know?

Radiocarbon dating is a scientific method of dating any material that was once living, such as bone. The radiocarbon method was developed by a team of scientists in America after the Second World War.

Key Evidence Found at Glenulra

- An oval-shaped stone enclosure wall.
- Entrance gap in enclosure wall.
- Post holes – holes in the ground where wooden posts would have been to hold up the house. The wooden structure of the house itself has not survived.
- A smaller, egg-shaped enclosure nearby may have been an animal pen.
- Charcoal within the enclosure, showing where fires were built for cooking – radiocarbon dated to a few centuries before 3000 BC.
- 76 pieces of broken pottery.
- Flakes of a stone called flint, the result of flint tools being made.
- A stone arrowhead and scrapers. Scrapers were tools used to work leather for use as clothing.
- A saddle quern – a smooth stone used for grinding wheat by rubbing a smaller stone on top.

History Detective

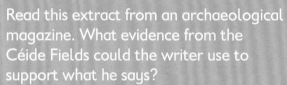

Read this extract from an archaeological magazine. What evidence from the Céide Fields could the writer use to support what he says?

'The Stone Age farmers who operated together to clear hundreds of acres of trees at the Céide Fields were a large, organised and peaceful community. Once cleared the Stone Age farmers divided the land into systems of fields. Their main living was from cattle rearing. However, they were also very skilled crafts people, working with both wood and stone. Their religious beliefs were important to them.'

Think and Discuss

1. Read through the key archaeological evidence found at the house site. What evidence suggests that a Stone Age family house might have been there?

2. What evidence tells us that these people were farmers?

3. What do the broken pieces of pottery tell us?

TIMELINE: THE CÉIDE FIELDS

3700 BC	3200 BC	AD 1930	AD 1970	AD 1993
Houses and field walls at Céide Fields are built	Fields are abandoned and blanket bog begins to form	Patrick Caulfield discovers the field walls	Excavation of the house site at Glenulra begins	Opening of the Céide Fields visitor centre

Lisa's Holiday House in Belderrig County Mayo

My father's family comes from a small village in North Mayo called Belderrig. It's a friendly place with a small local community where everyone knows everyone else. It is located a few miles down the coast from the Céide Fields visitor centre. My great-grandmother left her house in Belderrig to my father when she died. Some of the Stone Age field walls have been discovered on the hill right behind her house. Those ancient stone walls cover a bigger area of North Mayo than I thought. I sometimes wonder if they used stones from the ancient field walls to build the house. Her house is now our holiday home.

The great thing about this house is that my great-grandmother kept everything inside just as it was when she first lived there. Two of the old farm buildings are still there, but they are in ruins now. Sheep and cattle were once kept in them.

When my friends visited they thought it was very old-fashioned, but I love learning about it.

When you open the front door you walk into the main kitchen which is also the living room. There is no hallway. The only other rooms are two bedrooms, and there is a bathroom out the back. The bathroom was added in the 1960s. The floor of the house is made of stone. Dad says carpets would have been expensive in those days and hard to keep clean. For most of her life, my great-grandmother didn't have any electricity. We all love sitting by the big open turf fire. There is a large iron kettle hanging beside it.

A local historian stopped by one day and told us some of the history of the house. It was built just after the Great Famine in the 1840s. He knows this because he has seen the family name on townland records in the library going back to that time. He told us that according to local stories, the house was used to shelter rebels from the British forces in 1920.

I wondered where they could have hidden, the house is so small! The census records show that my great-grandmother was one of 10 children. We found an old black and white photo of them all as children. Six of them emigrated to the USA. That is why I have so many American cousins today.

The house is built from local stones. It has a thatched roof and the walls of the house are painted white, inside and out. Dad says that when his grandmother was a girl they were painted with whitewash, which was a cheap type of paint made from lime and chalk that farmers used.

Inside the house there are some really interesting old things. There is an old-fashioned sewing machine that works when you turn a handle in the side. Dad says his grandmother would make a lot of her own clothes. A milk churn stands by the door. After milking the cows, a wooden stick was used to mix the milk, up and down, to make butter.

My great-grandmother died a long time before I was born. I wish I could meet her to ask her questions about her life in Belderrig.

Think and Discuss

1. List the sources of evidence used by Lisa to tell the history of her family home in Belderrig. Find as many as you can.

2. How has the local area influenced how this house was built?

3. List three similarities between the way people lived in this house and the way of life in the Stone Age house in Glenulra.

Did You Know?

After the Great Famine, soda bread cooked on a griddle in the home became popular in Ireland. A griddle was a metal plate that hung over the open fire.

The Key to Literacy

Imagine that you are Lisa's great-grandmother living in Belderrig as a child in the 1920s. From what you have read, write a diary entry describing a day in her life.

My Book – The History of Mayo's Houses

Hi, I'm Noelle. I am a historian based in Ballina. I started writing a book about the history of houses in County Mayo after visiting the Stone Age house site in Glenulra in the Céide Fields. It made me realise just how long people have been making their home in County Mayo. I wanted to research examples of houses through the ages, and to see how they have changed over time. I looked at what size they were, what building materials were used, what furniture and other items would have been found inside them and how the local area influenced them.

I have studied everything from Stone Age house sites, to ring forts, tower houses, castles and more modern buildings also, all in County Mayo. They all have a story to tell.

I found a picture in a local library from the 1800s of the street in Ballina where I live. The town houses each side of my apartment building are still there, but in the photo I can see a house where my building now stands in its place. By reading local records I discovered that a writer lived in the house. Old maps of Mayo show where houses used to be. I have found that some large houses in Mayo started out as very small cottages. Talking to older people helps to get a sense of the changes that they have seen in houses over time. They remember things like the first time their house got electricity or a telephone. Some of the saddest things I found were the villages and houses that are now deserted and in ruins after the Great Famine.

Over to You

What sources of evidence did Noelle use to learn about the history of houses in Mayo? State whether each source is a primary or secondary source. If you were to study the houses of your local area, what sources of evidence do you think you could use?

Lesson Wrap-Up

Visual Summary

The Céide Fields is a Stone Age site in County Mayo. It contains field walls, houses and tombs dating back to 3000 BC. It was discovered by a local schoolteacher in the 1930s.

The house site at the Céide Fields provides evidence of Stone Age farmers. Another house in this chapter teaches us about the lives of people in Mayo after the Great Famine.

Writers and historians use many sources to research the history of houses in Ireland.

What Did I Learn?

What have I learned in this chapter?

What else would I like to know?

Where can I find this information?

Review

1. **Recall**

   When were the stone walls and houses at the Céide Fields built?

2. **Vocabulary**

   In this chapter we mentioned 'radiocarbon dating', a scientific way of dating a piece of material that was once living, such as a plant or bone. Find out what 'carbon' is and how it helps archaeologists to date things.

3. **Critical Thinking**

   A book on archaeology says that 'a small amount of domestic material was discovered at the Stone Age house site in Glenulra, County Mayo'. What do you think domestic material is?

4. **Be a Historian!**

   Write a report on a house that you find interesting in your local area. It can be from any period of history. It can even be your own house! Your investigation should use some of the historical sources mentioned in this lesson.

3 The First Emperor of China

What Will I Learn?

- About the Qin dynasty and the rule of the Emperor Qin Shi Huang.
- About what life was like for the people of China under the first emperor's rule.
- About places we can visit in China which date from this time.

Blog

Hello. My name is Chen Zhipeng and I'm a student at UCD in Dublin. I am studying history and, because of my Chinese roots, I have decided to focus my studies on the Qin dynasty in ancient China. A dynasty is a ruling family, and in ancient China most dynasties ruled for hundreds of years before being taken over by another dynasty. Dating from 221 BC to 207 BC, the Qin dynasty lasted only fifteen years!

The word Qin is pronounced like the English word 'chin'. It is where China gets its name from. My friends thought there wouldn't be enough to study about in the short Qin dynasty but I explained that they couldn't be more wrong. What the Emperor Qin Shi Huang managed to get done in those years is amazing. He brought the huge country of China together. He had unimaginable power and control over the Chinese people at that time. That doesn't mean that I agree with all of his ways of doing things! He was very strict and tough and expected everyone to do exactly what he wanted at all times.

As I study the life of the emperor I discover more and more interesting things. Next year I am planning to visit China and see with my own eyes some of the evidence of the Qin dynasty. I'm very excited to see the Terracotta Army. The photos I've seen of it are stunning.

Think and Discuss

1. Do you recognise anything in the photographs? Describe what you see in them.

2. Can you think of other famous people in history who had the kind of power and control that Emperor Qin Shi Huang had? When and where did they rule?

3. How would you describe the expression on the face of the emperor?

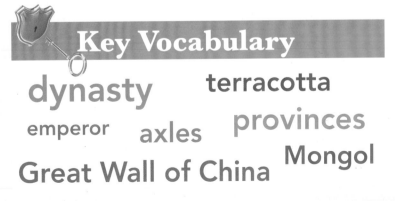

Key Vocabulary

dynasty   terracotta

emperor   axles   provinces

Great Wall of China   Mongol

Emperor Qin Shi Huang and the Qin Dynasty

Before the time of the Qin dynasty, over 2,000 years ago, China was made up of many states that were always at war with each other. One of these was called the state of Qin. In 247 BC a man called Ying Zheng became the king of the state of Qin when he was just 13 years old. As he became more powerful, more states fell under the control of his armies. Eventually in 221 BC King Zheng named himself the first emperor of China. He took the new name Qin Shi Huang. He felt that emperor was an even more powerful title than a king.

As well as being powerful, Qin Shi Huang was a very clever man. He had a lot of ideas about how China should be ruled. He wanted to rule all the different peoples of China as one big country and from one central place. He based himself in the city of Xianyang where he had huge palaces built for himself. It is said that he never slept in the same place twice. He didn't like his enemies to know where he was!

Did You Know?

The emperor wanted the people to follow his every command. He ordered the burning of all the books from the past that went against his laws. He killed any wise men and teachers who disagreed with his ideas. The books he burnt included poetry, stories and history books. He didn't burn books that he thought would help his empire to grow, such as books on medicine and farming.

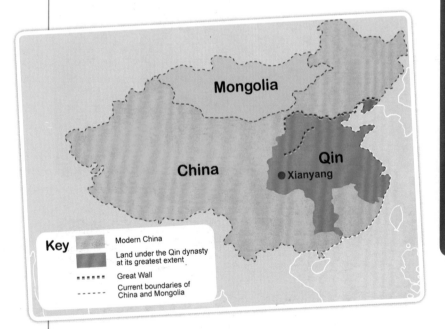

Mongolia

China

Qin

● Xianyang

Key

Modern China

Land under the Qin dynasty at its greatest extent

Great Wall

Current boundaries of China and Mongolia

Qin Shi Huang declares himself first emperor of China. Start of Qin dynasty
221 BC

Qin Shi Huang becomes king of the state of Qin
247 BC

Birth of Qin Shi Huang
259 BC

Qin Shi Huang was a great believer in laws. He thought that the only way to bring all the states of China together was to make everyone behave in the same way. He divided the empire into provinces. He had officials to look after the provinces, and controlled his empire with strict laws and harsh punishments.

He also made his people spy on each other. They had to expose anyone who was not obeying his laws. Anyone who refused to spy would face punishment or death. The emperor forced thousands of people to work at building some of his projects. He also put a set of rules in place to make sure that his dynasty would be able to easily rule China forever more.

End of Qin dynasty and the start of the Han dynasty.

206 BC

Death of Qin Shi Huang

210 BC

Book burnings are ordered by the emperor

213 BC

Checkpoint

1. When did King Zhen of Qin become Qin Shi Huang, the first emperor of China?

2. What city did the emperor rule from?

3. Name two things that the emperor expected his people to do.

History Detective

The Qin dynasty in China is not the only time in history that books were burned by people ruling a country. See if you can discover a time and place in the last 100 years when book burnings took place. Why did the ruler of that place order books to be burned?

Achievements of the Qin Dynasty

Many historians would describe the first emperor as a cruel leader. Written history shows that he felt he was helping his people. In the short time of the Qin dynasty he achieved some important things. As well as uniting the states of China he wanted them all to write in the same way. So a standard way of writing was put in place across all of China. He knew that this would help people from every part of the country to communicate and to do business with each other. He also made the way people use weights and measures the same.

For the same reason he wanted everyone to use the same money system. The same copper coins were put in use all over his empire. Unlike our coins in Ireland, these round coins had a square hole in the middle of them. This meant that coins could be kept together on a string to make bigger amounts.

As China was such a huge country, the emperor wanted people to be able to move easily from place to place. He set about building a large network of new roads. He made a law that the axles of carts, which ran across from wheel to wheel, were all to be of the same length. This meant they could run smoothly on his new roads and help to speed up the transport of goods and people. He also built new canals and bridges. Many of the emperor's improvements helped the economy of China.

Think About It

Qin Shi Huang is often described as a cruel and harsh ruler, forcing people to die by working them so hard on his huge building projects. The first emperor said "a thousand die so that a million may live." What, do you think, did he mean by that?

The Key to Literacy

Make two columns in your copybook. In one column write down the negative things that you think the first emperor did to his people. In the second column write down any positive things that you've learned about his rule.

Did You Know?

When Qin Shi Huang died there were two more Qin emperors, but they ruled for only five years between them. The people rose against the Qin Empire and the Han dynasty took over for the next 400 years.

Our Honeymoon in China
Blog

Hi everyone. Gavin and I are having such a great time in China. The two weeks since we saw you all at our wedding have flown by! Even though it was expensive to get here, we're so glad we've made this trip. I wanted to send you some pictures and tell you about two of the incredible historic sites we've seen.

Last week we saw the Great Wall of China. The Chinese worked on building this for 1,700 years! It started as a series of small walls that were not connected. The first emperor of China, Qin Shi Huang, made huge improvements to it. He made it stronger and wider. He wanted to build the best barricade possible against Mongol invaders from the north. Every emperor after him added their own pieces to the wall.

We felt sorry for the poor peasants and the captured people who were put to work on it. It was back breaking work and they weren't paid — they were slaves. Workers were killed by falling rocks and died of disease and exhaustion. They were only fed enough to keep them alive. The wall is amazing. It is so big that it can be seen from space!

Yesterday we went to see the Terracotta Army near the city of Xi'an. The same emperor I mentioned, Qin Shi Huang, wanted to rule even after his death. While he was still alive he ordered the construction of his own tomb. Beside it he wanted a whole army made out of clay buried with him so that he could continue to rule after he died.

They made 6,000 life-size soldiers out of red terracotta clay! That emperor must have been one of the most powerful men who ever lived. You can also see spears, chariots and horses made of clay. No two soldiers look alike. Some of the soldiers were kneeling on the ground, about to shoot terracotta bows. We were only allowed to look at them from a balcony. The tour guide told us that these soldiers are very important to the Chinese people. Only important visitors, like the Queen of England, have been allowed to walk among them and see them up close.

Checkpoint

1. Why was the Great Wall of China built?

2. What was the name of the emperor's enemies to the north?

3. How many terracotta soldiers were buried at the site near Xi'an?

Research and Write It

The Terracotta Army of Qin Shi Huang was discovered in 1974 by some local Chinese farmers. They were digging a well in the ground. The first thing they saw was the top of a clay head. Imagine that you are one of those farmers. Write an entry in your diary about that exciting day. Describe what you found as you continued to dig. Look at photographs of the Terracotta Army to help you.

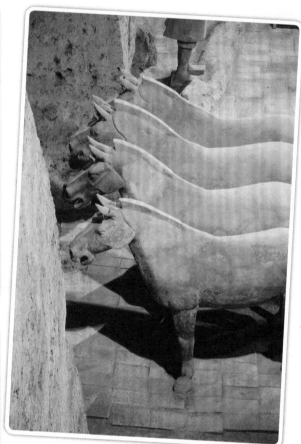

Over to You

1. Find some information about another famous wall from another part of the world – Hadrian's Wall. Where was this wall built? When was it built? Why was it built?

2. The tomb of the powerful pharaoh Tutankhamun was discovered in 1922. Research some of the objects that were buried with this pharaoh in the belief that he could use them after he died.

Did You Know?

A small selection of the Terracotta Army has been shown at museum exhibitions around the world, in places like London, England and Barcelona, Spain.

Lesson Wrap-Up

Qin Dynasty

Review

1. **Recall**

   Why did coins in the Qin Empire have square holes in the middle of them?

2. **Vocabulary**

   Explain the difference between the words 'king' and 'emperor'. Put them both into sentences to show that you understand what they mean.

3. **Critical Thinking**

   If you had to justify the harsh rule of Qin Shi Huang for a class debate, what would you say?

4. **Be a Historian!**

   The ancient Chinese invented many things that are still in use today. These include silk, paper, printing, wheelbarrows, wallpaper, ink, kites, playing cards and gunpowder. Choose one invention that China has given us. Find out about the history of that invention and how it is used today. Design a colourful poster which tells the story of that invention and why it is still important today.

4 Creatures and Myths

What Will I Learn?

- About mythological creatures from different cultures.
- About the legends of the banshee, the dullahan, Medusa and the phoenix.
- How myths and legends tell us a lot about the beliefs and values of people from the past.
- How to recognise elements of fantasy and exaggeration in mythology.

Think and Discuss

1. Do you recognise any of these mythical creatures? What are they?

2. Where have you heard of these mythical creatures before?

3. What other mythical creatures can you think of? What do you know about them?

4. Are there any mythical creatures associated with Ireland? Name them.

Key Vocabulary

banshee   lament

phoenix   dullahan

mortal

Medusa   gorgons

Mythical Irish Creatures

Stories about mythical Irish creatures, like the banshee and the dullahan, give us a good idea of people's attitudes to death and magic in old Ireland.

The Dullahan

The dullahan is a headless horseman from the Irish fairy kingdom. This terrifying creature is said to carry its own head in its right hand. Legend has it that the repulsive head glows with decay and wears a hideous, idiotic grin. People believed that the dullahan rode through the countryside using his head as a lantern in search of dying people. Those who claimed to see the creature said he used a human spine as a whip for his black horse.

According to myth, the dullahan could speak only once on each journey. He would stop at a house and call the name of a dying person to summon their soul. Some people believed that the dullahan was afraid of gold and used it to drive him away. The dullahan is believed to have originated from the Celtic god, Crom Dubh, who was worshipped in Ireland until the sixth century.

The Banshee

The banshee has been part of Ireland's mythology since the Middle Ages. According to legend, this female spirit is an angel of death. Generations of Irish people have told stories of a ghostly woman who wails in the dead of night. Some say the banshee appears as a beautiful young woman, others say she is a frightening old hag in a dark hooded cloak. Many claim that she can take the form of a crow, hare, stoat or weasel – animals associated with witchcraft. The creature is most famous for her distinctive cry which warns people of a death in the family which is about to occur.

Depending on where you live, you may hear different descriptions of her cry. In Leinster, the banshee's wail is said to be so piercing it can shatter glass. Kerry people describe a low, pleasant singing while people from Antrim recorded hearing a screeching sound. Historically, many believed that the banshee punished the souls of sinners and protected those who had lived good lives.

Think and Discuss

1. Does the story of the dullahan sound believable to you? Pick out all the parts which you think could be fantasy or exaggeration.

2. From reading the legend of the banshee, what things do you think people believed about death and magic?

Did You Know?

The Banshee is linked to an old Irish tradition called 'caoineadh', or the 'keen', which meant to lament. Women sang laments at funerals. People in the village heard the songs and knew someone had died.

Medusa

The ancient Greek sea gods, Ceto and Phorcys, had three daughters. Two of the girls were immortal monsters known as gorgons. This meant that they could not die. The youngest daughter, Medusa, was mortal. Medusa was considered the most beautiful woman in Athens and was well aware of her own good looks. She often boasted about her long golden hair and green eyes and spent a lot of time gazing at her own reflection.

One day Medusa visited the Parthenon, a temple that had been built for the goddess Athena. The temple was decorated with sculptures and paintings of Athena. Medusa remarked that she was much more beautiful than Athena. She said that someday people would probably build a temple to worship her. This angered Athena greatly and she decided to strip Medusa of her beauty. She appeared before Medusa and said, 'Beauty fades in all mortals! I shall punish you for your vanity and make an example of you. This will teach other mortals to control their pride.'

Think About It

What emotions do you think Athena was feeling before she placed a curse on Medusa?

Athena turned Medusa into a gorgon. Her face became that of a hideous monster, her skin became scaly and her hair coiled into several hissing snakes. Athena also placed a curse on Medusa, saying 'From this day on, any man who looks into your eyes will turn to stone!'

Medusa was then cast down to live with her gorgon sisters in a cave, away from people. She became a very angry monster with a deep hatred for humans. Many men visited the cave to look upon or slay Medusa but all turned to stone when they looked into her eyes.

One day, the hero Perseus was given a reflective shield and winged sandals by the gods Athena and Hermes, to retrieve the head of Medusa. When Perseus reached the cave, he found men and animals made of stone. He used the shield as a mirror to avoid looking Medusa in the eye and cut off her head.

From that day the head of Medusa was used in many battles, to turn enemies into stone.

Design and Draw

Draw a comic strip to retell the story of Medusa. Show the events in the correct order.

Key to Literacy

Write a short story about a mythical creature. The creature may be one you invent yourself or one you have heard of in other myths and legends. Don't be afraid to exaggerate and bend the truth. Myths are full of fantasy!

The Phoenix

The Egyptian sun god heard a magnificent song. He looked down and saw a bird as big as an eagle, with feathers the colour of sunrise. Realising that this bird was the only one of its kind, the sun god decided to give it eternal life. A hundred years passed and mankind named this bird 'the phoenix'. They began trying to capture the bird and so it decided to fly away to a hidden island.

The phoenix lived peacefully on the island for 500 years, singing songs. Over time, it grew old and asked the sun to make it young again. When there was no reply, the phoenix decided to go home. On the way, it gathered leaves and tree bark. It landed on the top of the palm tree where it had once lived and built a nest. It used myrrh from a nearby tree to make an egg. It sat down and prayed, "Make me young and strong again".

The sun began to shine so brightly that all of the other animals had to hide from its rays. The phoenix basked in the heat until it became a huge ball of fire. When the flames finally stopped, it was gone and all that remained was a pile of grey ash.

A young phoenix rose up out of the ash and grew until it was as big as the old phoenix. It poured the ashes into the egg shell. The clouds returned to the sky and all the other animals came out of hiding. The Phoenix placed the egg on the altar of the Egyptian temple of the sun, before flying off to the desert.

According to legend, every 500 years, when the phoenix has grown old again, it flies back to nest at the top of a palm tree and waits for the sun to turn it to ashes. Each time, a young phoenix rises from the ashes.

Did You Know?

The Phoenix can be found in the folklore of many cultures. There are versions of this legend in Egypt, China, Japan, Arabia, Russia and America.

Think About It

How, do you think, did the first humans in the story feel when they saw the magnificent Phoenix? Why did they want to capture it?

Over to You

Retell the story of the phoenix in your own words. Put the events of the story in the correct order.

Research and Write It

Research the story of the phoenix across two different cultures. Write a short essay to compare and contrast the details of each story. Discuss the forms of expression used in each story.

Lesson Wrap-Up

Visual Summary

Myths and legends use exaggeration and fantasy to tell a story. Irish legends mention mythical creatures such as the banshee and the dullahan.

Medusa is a Greek legend about a beautiful woman who was punished for her vanity. The goddess Athena cursed Medusa so that her looks were transformed and any man who looked at her turned to stone.

The legend of the phoenix tells the story of a majestic bird who dies and rises from the ashes. There are variations of this myth to be found in several cultures.

Review

1. **Recall**

   What did the people of Leinster say about the cry of the Banshee?

2. **Vocabulary**

   Think of another word for each of the following: vanity, mythical, piercing and repulsive.

3. **Critical Thinking**

   Do you feel pity for any of the creatures in this lesson? If so, which ones and why?

4. **Be a Historian!**

   For each of the myths in this chapter, state which parts of the myths you think might be believable and which parts are not believable. Also write down where you might find more information about each myth.

What Did I Learn?

What have I learned in this chapter?

What else would I like to know?

Where can I find this information?

5 The Aztecs

- Who the Aztec people were and when they lived.
- About life in Aztec society.
- About the importance of religion and gods to the Aztecs.
- How the Aztec Empire came to an end.

The Aztecs were a race of people who lived where the country of Mexico is today. Their civilisation lasted from about AD 1250 till AD 1521. Look at the map of the Aztec Empire. The part of Mexico that the Aztecs lived on is the strip of land that connects North America with South America. They may have settled here after leaving lands in the north where there was famine and drought. An Aztec legend suggests that the Aztec people wandered through the desert for many years.

They built their capital city, Tenochtitlan, on an island in Lake Texcoco. Today, the capital city of Mexico, Mexico City, is built in the same place. The original Lake Texcoco was drained in an effort to control flooding in the seventeenth century. Mexico City is built on the drained lake basin.

We know something about how the Aztecs lived from ruins of buildings, remains of pottery, jewellery, and other artefacts that have been found. We also have the writings of the first Europeans to see the Aztec people. Aztecs were fierce warriors and fought many neighbouring tribes in battle to build their great empire.

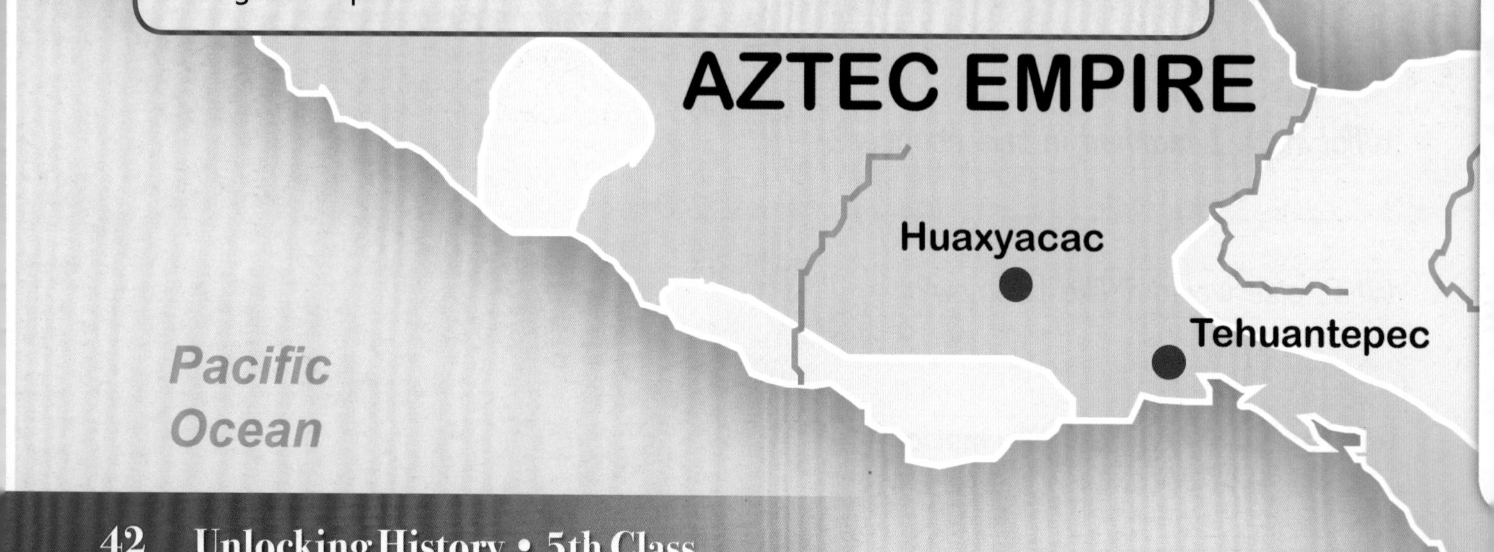

Gulf of Mex

AZTEC EMPIRE

Huaxyacac

Tehuantepec

Pacific
Ocean

Think and Discuss

1. Locate Mexico on a map of the world. Describe its location.

2. Describe the Aztec buildings shown in the photograph below. What do you think they were used for?

3. What was happening in Ireland at the time of the Aztec Empire, do you think?

Key Vocabulary

Aztecs irrigation maize

hieroglyphics

sacrifice

codex

conquistadors solstice

Life in Aztec Times

Most Aztec people were farmers. They also fished and hunted for food. They did not have horses or ploughs or even wheels, but they grew plenty of food to eat. The Aztecs were a clever people. They made the most of whatever land they had. They dug channels in the ground in dry areas to bring water for crops, a process called irrigation. They built floating gardens in lakes to grow food on. They grew vegetables and fruit like tomatoes and avocados. They slept on rush mats and made their own clothes from cotton. Maize was the most important food crop that the Aztecs grew. It was eaten at every meal. They made it into flour which was used to make pancakes which were stuffed with a variety of fillings. They kept turkeys but had no pigs, sheep or cattle.

▲ Aztec farmers building floating gardens

The Aztec Empire was ruled by a king. The next most important people were the city rulers, war leaders and nobles. Beneath them were the ordinary people. At the lowest level of Aztec society were the slaves.

Ordinary people wore simple clothes made from cotton or cloth made from a cactus plant. Only Aztecs from the richer levels of society were allowed to wear jewellery and colourful costumes, which showed how powerful they were. Aztec priests wore large headdresses made from feathers. The rich people had slaves to work for them.

Rich people lived in bigger houses built of stone or bricks, built around a patio. These homes usually had several separate buildings, including a place for steam baths. Meanwhile, many farmers lived in mud-brick houses. The Aztecs wanted their citizens to behave correctly. They wrote down the laws that people had to follow. Children were taught correct behaviour in schools, which all children had to attend. These schools taught children how to be engineers, builders and traders, important jobs which would help the Aztec Empire to grow.

▲ A modern recreation of an Aztec ceremonial costume

Fact File

Ullamaliztli – An Aztec Ball Game

- Ullamaliztli was a popular Aztec ball game.

- It was played on a ball court. Players had to get the ball through a carved stone hoop that was over three metres above the court.

- It was played with a rubber ball. The name of the game comes from the word 'ulli' meaning rubber. The Aztecs got their rubber from rubber trees.

- The game was difficult to play and very important to the Aztecs, not only for sport but also for politics and religion.

- The best ballplayers were treated like stars in Aztec society.

Checkpoint

1. Explain what irrigation means.

2. Which group was at the lowest level of Aztec society?

3. What were homes in Aztec times made from?

4. Name two important jobs in Aztec times.

Did You Know?

The Aztecs were among the first people in the world to make chocolate. The richer members of Aztec society could enjoy a hot drink they called 'xocoatl' which later became known as 'chocolatl'. It was made by grinding down cacao beans. When Spanish explorers brought chocolate back to Europe it was found to be too bitter so honey was added to sweeten it.

Research and Write It

What sort of things do you think would have been taught in an Aztec school? Do some research in your library or online. Now write out an imaginary school timetable showing a plan of what Aztec children would be taught each day of the week.

Aztec Religious Beliefs

The Aztec people were very religious. They believed in many powerful gods. They believed that their gods caused the sun to rise, the crops to grow and the rain to fall. Aztec priests and priestesses held a very high place in society. As well as their religious role, they were teachers, artists, writers, scientists, historians and doctors. They knew about astronomy, which is the study of the stars in the night sky. They also understood and studied numbers. Priests lived in the temple buildings. Aztec temples looked like a set of giant stone steps which were pyramid in shape. The temples also had special gardens and pools for the priests to pray and wash in.

▲ A statue of Tlaloc, the Aztec god of rain

The Aztecs feared if they did not keep the gods happy they would be destroyed. They offered their gods human blood, which meant sacrificing people. Those chosen for sacrifice were often prisoners from Aztec wars. The killing was done at the top of the temple building. The Aztecs believed that by giving the gods blood the sun would continue to rise and their lives could continue as normal. For this reason the sun god was the most important to them. Aztecs had a strong belief in the afterlife. They believed that a person who was sacrificed would go straight to live with the gods.

The Aztecs planned their religious ceremonies around their calendar. The calendar consisted of a 365-day year, like our own calendar. This showed how closely the Aztec people followed the movement of the earth, sun and stars. The calendar was displayed on a circular stone. Solstice days, the longest and shortest days of the year, were of special importance. Aztec priests used the calendar to find the luckiest

▲ An Aztec calendar

days for such things as when to build houses, plant crops, and go into battle. A big festival took place every 52 years called the New Fire Ceremony. Everyone allowed the fires in their houses to go out. Then they would light their fires again from a new fire that the priests would light in the temple. This was followed by a huge feast.

The Aztecs drew and carved images of their gods. They used symbol writing known as hieroglyphics to tell the stories of their gods, just like the ancient Egyptians did.

Fact File

▲ *Quetzalcoatl*

Aztec Gods

- The head of the gods was **Huitzilopochtli**, god of war and god of sun. Aztec legend says that this god led the people to the place where they built their capital city, Tenochtitlan.

- **Tlaloc** was the Aztec rain god. He also controlled storms, thunder and lightning. This god was very important to Aztec farmers.

- **Quetzalcoatl** was a feathered snake who represented arts, crafts, learning and knowledge. He was very important to Aztec priests.

Think and Discuss

1. The Aztec stone calendar was displayed in a circle shape. How are calendars that we use today different?

2. How are hieroglyphics different from the letters that we use to write with?

Design and Draw

The Aztecs created some very interesting and striking images of their gods. Find a picture or a description of an Aztec god and use it to create a design for a t-shirt to be sold to tourists at a historic site in Mexico.

3. Why would the god Quetzalcoatl be especially important to Aztec priests?

4. Why would the god Tlaloc be important to Aztec farmers?

Did You Know?

The Aztecs had a system of writing which they wrote down in books which folded like a fan. These books were called codices. A single book was called a codex. They were hand-written on paper. They all contained pictures of things like calendars, masks, rituals and ceremonies.

The Key to Literacy
Summarising

Reread the section about the religious beliefs of the Aztecs. What are the main points of information? Summarise the key information using bullet points.

The Arrival of the Spanish

When the Aztec Empire was at its most successful, explorers from Europe arrived. In 1519, a Spanish man named Hernán Cortes sailed his ships into the Gulf of Mexico. Cortes and his men were conquistadors – Spanish soldiers, adventurers and explorers. When they landed, Cortes ordered that the ships they had travelled in be burnt. This was to stop his men from deserting him.

At first, the Aztecs were scared of the conquistadors who had horses, dogs and cannons. The Aztecs had never seen such things before and believed that Cortes and his men might have come from the gods and gave them gifts and welcomed them. The Aztecs soon realised that this was not the case.

▲ Hernán Cortes

As conquistadors, Hernán Cortes and his men had a mission. They were looking for lands to conquer, gold to take and people to convert to the Catholic religion. The conquistadors realised that there were great riches to be had in the Aztec lands.

In 1520, the Aztecs drove the conquistadors out of their capital city, Tenochtitlan, after a long battle. The Aztecs were angry with their leader, Montezuma II, for welcoming the conquistadors to their kingdom and they killed him. He was the last ever Aztec leader.

The conquistadors returned in 1521 and invited local tribes who were enemies of the Aztecs to join them. These tribes took this opportunity to get even with the Aztecs and helped the Spanish to destroy them. Even though they were fierce warriors, the Aztecs were no match for the Spanish invaders.

▲ Hernán Cortes meets Montezuma II

After a long battle between the Aztecs and the conquistadors, Tenochtitlan was destroyed. The Spanish rebuilt the city as Mexico City. This became the capital of New Spain, the name the conquistadors gave to their newly conquered land. Today, there are thought to be up to a million people who are descended from the Aztec people living in Mexico.

Research and Write It

Read the following quote from the writings of a Spanish conquistador named Bernal Diaz del Castillo:

'All about us we saw cities and villages built in the water, their great towers and buildings of masonry rising out of it... When I beheld the scenes around me I thought within myself, this was the garden of the world.'

Imagine that you are Bernal and you are writing a letter to your family back in Spain. From what you know about Aztec society, describe the sights you have seen and how the Aztec people reacted to the Spanish. For example, the Aztecs had never seen horses before.

Did You Know?

One of the best weapons the Spanish conquistadors brought with them was disease, such as measles. The Aztecs had never had to cope with these diseases before and many thousands of them died.

Checkpoint

1. What was the name of the Spanish conquistador who brought the Aztec Empire under Spanish control?

2. What were conquistadors?

3. Who was the last Aztec leader? Why, do you think, is 'II' is put after his name?

4. What new name did the Spanish give to the Aztec lands?

Think and Discuss

1. What sort of people do you think the conquistadors were? Give reasons for your answer.

2. Do you think you would like the job of a conquistador? Why?/Why not?

3. Do you think the Aztecs were right to kill their leader, Montezuma II? Give a reason for your answer.

4. Why do you think the name 'New Spain' was given to the Aztec lands? Do you like this name? Why?/Why not?

TIMELINE

AD 1100

Aztecs leave their homeland searching for a new home

Aztecs arrive in Mexico

AD 1195

AD 1250

Aztecs settle near Lake Texcoco

Tenochtitlan, the capital city of the Aztecs, is built

AD 1325

AD 1400

Aztec Empire expands

Montezuma II becomes ruler. Aztec Empire at its largest size

AD 1502

AD 1519

Hernán Cortes arrives from Spain

Montezuma II is killed

AD 1520

AD 1521

Tenochtitlan destroyed

Tenochtitlan rebuilt, re-named Mexico City, capital of the Spanish colony of New Spain

AD 1522

Lesson Wrap-Up

Visual Summary

The Aztec Empire lasted from AD 1250 to AD 1521 where the country of Mexico is today.

They worshipped many gods and made human sacrifices to them. They had a calendar based on the movement of the sun, moon and stars.

Spanish conquistadors, led by Hernán Cortes, arrived in AD 1519 and claimed Aztec lands for Spain. By 1522 the territory of New Spain was in place, marking the end of the Aztec Empire.

What Did I Learn?

What have I learned in this chapter?

What else would I like to know?

Where can I find this information?

Review

1. **Recall**

   Name one of the Aztec gods and describe what they represented.

2. **Vocabulary**

   'Conquistador' comes from the Spanish word meaning 'to conquer'. Find a definition for the word 'conquer' and use the word in a sentence about the Aztecs.

3. **Critical Thinking**

   Evaluate the reasons that the Spanish had for wanting to claim the Aztec lands. Do you think they were good reasons?

4. **Be a Historian!**

   The Mayan people were another, older civilisation that lived to the south of the Aztec Empire. For a few hundred years the two civilisations existed side by side. Find out what you can about how the Mayans lived. What similarities were there between the Mayans and the Aztecs? How were they different?

6 Education and Schools

What Will I Learn?

- About the history of education and schools in Ireland.
- How to look at sources of evidence relating to schools in the past.
- About the changes that have taken place in schools over time.

Read this description of a hedge school taken from *'Traits and Stories of the Irish Peasantry'*, a series of short stories by William Carleton written in 1843.

'… a circle of urchins, sitting on the bare earth, stones, and hassocks, and exhibiting a series of speckled shins, all radiating towards the fire, like sausages on a Poloni dish. There they are – wedged as close as they can sit; one with half a thigh off his breeches – another with half an arm off his tattered coat – a third without breeches at all, wearing, as a substitute, a piece of his mother's old petticoat, pinned about his loins – a fourth, no coat – a fifth, with a cap on him, because he has got a scald, from having sat under the juice of fresh hung bacon – a sixth with a black eye – a seventh two rags about his heels to keep his kibes clean – an eighth crying to get home, because he had got a headache, though it may be as well to hint, that there is a drag-hunt to start from beside his father's in the course of the day.

In this ring, with his legs stretched in a most lordly manner, sits, upon a deal chair, Mat himself, with his hat on, basking in the enjoyment of unlimited authority. His dress consists of a black coat, considerably in want of repair, transferred to his shoulders through the means of a clothes-broker in the county town; a white cravat, round a large stuffing, having that part which comes in contact with the chin somewhat streaked with brown – a black waistcoat, with one or two 'tooth-an'-egg' metal buttons sewed on where the original had fallen off – black corduroy inexpressibles, twice dyed, and sheep's-gray stockings. In his hand is a large, broad ruler, the emblem of his power, the woeful instrument of executive justice, and the signal of terror to all within his jurisdiction.'

Think and Discuss

1. What do you think a hedge school is?

2. What type of person was the teacher? List some words to describe his personality.

3. How did the author describe the children?

4. How is this school different from your school?

5. When did hedge schools exist, do you think?

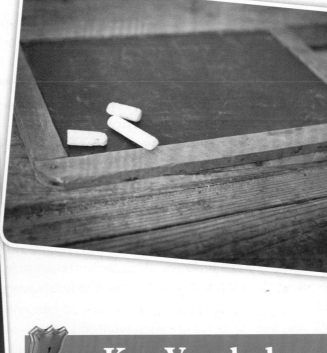

Key Vocabulary

re-enact   petticoat   cravat

emblem

mandatory   denominational

mission statement   dunces

A History of Schools in Ireland

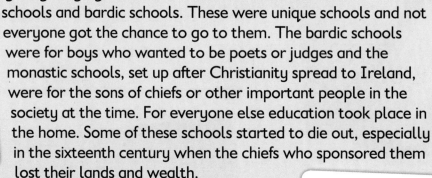

My name is Professor Carmel Mulvany. I teach Irish history in a university in America; my area of expertise is education in Ireland. There is a long tradition of education and schooling in Ireland. Often the types of schools present in an era can tell us a lot about that time. I will take you on a whistle-stop tour of Irish education and by doing so hopefully you will learn about Irish history too.

I'll start the journey long long ago when there were monastic schools and bardic schools. These were unique schools and not everyone got the chance to go to them. The bardic schools were for boys who wanted to be poets or judges and the monastic schools, set up after Christianity spread to Ireland, were for the sons of chiefs or other important people in the society at the time. For everyone else education took place in the home. Some of these schools started to die out, especially in the sixteenth century when the chiefs who sponsored them lost their lands and wealth.

Over the years Ireland became more influenced by neighbouring Britain. The reigns of different royals brought changes to schools and education. For example the Tudors wanted to make Ireland more like England and so they planned to set up a school in each parish in Ireland to teach people English customs and language. Parish diocesan and royal schools were all examples of schooling in Ireland during the reign of the Tudors.

▲ *Portora Royal School, Enniskillen*

The Penal Laws were introduced in Ireland by the British in the late seventeenth century. They were introduced to discriminate against the Catholics. Catholics were not allowed to attend Catholic schools and had to become members of the Church of Ireland if they wanted to go to school. Similarly, Catholic teachers were not allowed to teach and they could be fined if they were caught teaching. In response to these harsh laws against Catholics many secret schools were set up. They were called hedge schools or pay schools because they often took place in hedges and you had to pay to attend them. Payment often included food or turf.

An organisation called 'The Kildare Place Society' later set up charity schools to educate the poor people of Ireland. Next the British Government introduced free national schools in 1831 to educate children of all faiths between the ages of six and 12. While initially they were meant to educate children from all faiths, they eventually became denominational and were run by religious orders.

Religious orders include the Christian Brothers, Sisters of Mercy, Presentation Sisters and so on.

In the last number of years a wide variety of schools have been established in Ireland. For example, schools have been founded by non-Christian religious groups, e.g. Muslim and Jewish organisations. Other schools such as the Educate Together and VEC (Vocational Educational Committee) schools were founded by groups with a multi-denominational ethos. In the 2000s many people immigrated to Ireland and the population became very diverse. These schools reflect the diversity of society in Ireland today.

▲ Christian Brothers School, Youghal

Think About It

1. What were the Penal Laws?

2. Did the Penal Laws change education in Ireland? In what ways?

3. Name three ways that schooling has changed since the establishment of the National School system in 1831.

4. Why, do you think, are many schools in Ireland denominational?

Fact File

Schooling in Ireland

- In 1841 more than half of the Irish population could neither read nor write.
- The Irish Education Act of 1892 made education in Ireland free and mandatory for all children aged between six and 14.
- By 1901 only 14% of the Irish population could neither read nor write.
- In 1966 secondary school education was made free to every pupil in Ireland.

Date It

Look at the list below. As a class, try to find out when each of these types of schools were set up. Add these dates and some facts and figures to a classroom display on schooling in Ireland.

Bardic schools | Monastic schools | Parish schools | Diocesan schools | Royal schools | Hedge schools | Charity schools | National School System | Denominational schools | Multi-denominational schools | Non-denominational schools

The Changing Classroom

Classrooms, like schools in general, reflect changes over time. For example, in the past many classrooms were heated by fires. Today, many classrooms have heaters instead, as many homes do today. Look around your classroom. What aspects of your classroom would have been different 50 years ago, or 100 years ago?

Look closely at the photographs from the past and the photographs from modern classrooms. What can you see?

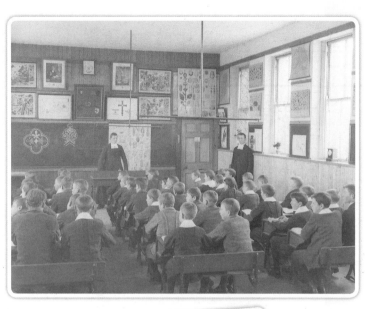

Think About It

1. When do you think the modern classroom photographs were taken?

2. How are the modern photographs different from the black and white photograph of a classroom? How are they similar?

3. How do you think your classroom will be different in 10 years' time?

4. What would you like classrooms to be like in 20 years' time?

History Detective

1. Name three similarities and three differences between the black and white picture of the classroom shown here and your classroom.

2. Can you be sure that this is a classroom from the past? Give reasons for your answer.

3. What do you think the bars hanging from the ceiling are used for in the classrom?

My School Project

Our class | **History** | **Geography**

Hi! We're the blue group reporting back to the world about our school project. We investigated the history of our school. Here's what we did.

First of all we brainstormed the topic. We all knew different things and had different ideas about our project. Darragh's dad works in the school so Darragh decided he would ask him questions about the history of the school. We prepared some interview questions together and decided we would record the interview so we could upload it later on if we wanted to.

Triona is great on computers so she used the internet to research the school. She got us into the school webpage. There we found out that our school was originally built in 1942 in a different location but it needed to expand in the late Sixties so it moved to a larger site. We also looked up our school in a search engine and found some photographs of it there.

Kyle decided he would make a book about the school. He wrote an introduction about the school and included our mission statement – we asked the principal for that. He also drew some pictures of the building, listed well known past pupils and included the text of some of the interview. Jenny and Kirsty went to the school library to see if they could find old school books from years ago. They wanted to make a timeline of books used in our school. Sometimes it was hard to tell which books were older but our teacher told us that the year they were printed is usually on the inside cover of the book. They also saw some of the first computers that came into the school – how things have changed. We now have laptops for everyone!

When we presented our project to the class we also tried to re-enact a school day from the past. One of us wore a uniform similar to the school uniform that was introduced in the 1950s. It was different from the one we wear today. It had different colours and a different crest. When researching the school uniform we found an old rule book that said that boys' hair had to be short. A few of the boys with long hair in the class looked worried. Interestingly, it also said that girls' hair couldn't be too short.

1 | 2

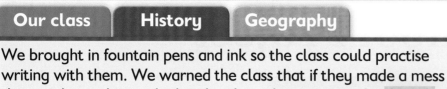

We brought in fountain pens and ink so the class could practise writing with them. We warned the class that if they made a mess they might get hit on the hand with a ruler or put in the dunce's corner – we wouldn't really have done that but Darragh's father said that years ago teachers did do things like that. Imagine!

Thanks for reading our blog!!

The blue group ☺

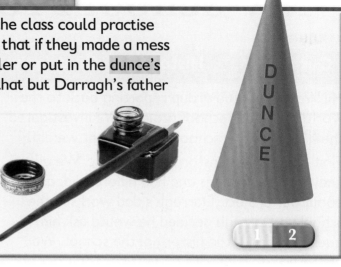

1 | 2

Checkpoint

1. What sources of evidence did the blue group use in their project?

2. How can you find out the age of a book?

3. How did the group present the project to their class? Was this a good way of presenting history?

Over to You

In groups, design a project on the history of learning in your own school, e.g. what did teachers use to teach with in the past, what did children write with, etc. Try to use as many different sources of evidence as you can to present your project to the class in an interesting way.

The Key to Literacy
Questioning

Write a set of questions that you will use to interview someone about the history of your school, e.g. the principal, a past pupil, a local historian, etc. Remember, if you want to get a person talking you need to ask questions that do not just have a yes or no answer.

Lesson Wrap-Up

Visual Summary

Ireland's history of schooling has included various types of schools such as monastic schools, hedge schools, charity schools and national schools.

Classrooms have changed a lot over the years. In the past, classrooms had fireplaces and pupils wrote on slates or with pens dipped into ink jars.

There are many ways to research your school's history, e.g. looking for evidence within your school, interviewing people, or checking the school library.

What Did I Learn?

What have I learned in this chapter?

What else would I like to know?

Where can I find this information?

Review

1. **Recall**

   What sources of evidence could you use to find out about the history of your school?

2. **Vocabulary**

   Draw a picture of each of the following items of clothing: breeches, petticoat, cravat. Remember to label each item.

3. **Critical Thinking**

   In what ways has being a teacher changed through the years? List at least three things about the job of a teacher that has changed.

4. **Be a Historian!**

   Research the East Wall schoolboys' strike in Dublin or any other student led protest that occurred in Irish history. Prepare a short presentation on your research. In your presentation explain how you carried out your research and what you found out.

7 The Famine

What Will I Learn?

- What caused the famine in Ireland in the 1840s.
- About the impact of the famine on Irish people.
- How the famine caused many long-term changes to life in Ireland.
- How the famine led to mass emigration to Britain and America.

1. Describe what you see in each photo.

2. What do you think happened to the cottage?

3. How do you think the ship in the photograph is linked to the famine?

4. What does the word 'famine' mean to you?

5. Which of these pictures are likely to be primary sources and which are likely to show secondary sources? Give reasons for your choices.

Key Vocabulary

famine   starvation   blight

tenants

workhouse   emigration

evicted

emigrants   cargo

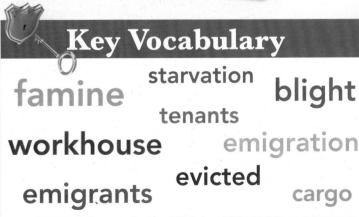

The Great Hunger

A famine is a severe shortage of food that can result in widespread starvation. Over the course of Irish history there have been many famines. However, the potato famine or 'Great Hunger' in the 1840s greatly affected the course of Irish history.

Here is an account of the famine through the eyes of a young girl, living in Ireland in 1846.

The year is 1846. Last year a terrible disease known as blight destroyed our potato crops. The potatoes went black and withered in the fields. Within a few months the people in my village began to feel the effects of the crop failure. Food became scarce and food prices rose.

In the spring, people planted more potatoes than ever before. Alas, the potato crops are failing again this year. People are eating whatever they can find. My family survives by eating fish, berries and seaweed.

Landlords are forcing poor families to leave their homes if they cannot afford to pay the high rents. They often have nowhere else to go and have to live on the side of the road. Our elderly neighbour, Mrs Graney, was evicted last week. She had an awful fever and nobody would take her in. She lay down on the side of the road and didn't get up again. Mother said she didn't have the energy to carry on.

Some families travel to the workhouse in the neighbouring town looking for a place to stay. Others are leaving the countryside in droves, searching for food and work in the cities.

Checkpoint

1. What happened to the potato crop during the famine?

2. What food is this family surviving on?

3. Why did landlords force their tenants to leave their homes?

Think About It

1. Describe how you think an evicted family would feel after being forced to leave their home. How would the parents feel? How would the children feel?

2. What types of food could a family with no potatoes and no money left gather for free?

Research and Write It

Find out more about life in the workhouses during the famine. Why did people go to workhouses? What was daily life like in a workhouse? Were there any workhouses in your area? Write a report on your research.

What Caused the Famine in Ireland

Before the start of the famine in 1845, the population of Ireland reached eight million people. Most were poor farmers who rented land from landlords. The land was divided into large estates and often owned by Protestant landlords.

Those who worked the land grew crops like oats and barley, and most of the harvest from these crops had to be given to the landlords as rent. The crops were then sold overseas.

The farmers fed themselves by growing potatoes, a nutritious crop that was cheap to grow. However in 1845, a potato blight quickly spread across Ireland. It was caused by a fungus called 'Phytophthora Infestans' and destroyed the potato crop. By the following spring, many people had run out of food. The British Prime Minister Robert Peel shipped £100,000 worth of cheap Indian corn to Ireland. But most Irish people did not know how to cook this, and the yellow porridge they created made them sick.

▲ *Robert Peel*

The British government believed it was better to give people paid work than hand out charity. This often meant hard labour building roads or piers. Others entered workhouses. In workhouses people worked all day long in return for food and shelter.

The potato crop failed again in 1846. The new government in Britain told Irish landlords that it was up to them to feed the poor people on their land. Many tenants had no money to pay their rent. Some landlords paid their tenants to leave the country, or emigrate. Others simply forced them out, or evicted them.

▲ *Starving people outside a workhouse*

Over to You

The Society of Friends (the Quakers) believed it was their duty to help the poor. They opened soup kitchens in many areas and handed out clothing. Have you ever heard about a famine or disaster in another country and wanted to help? Write a list of things that you could do to raise money.

Overview of the Famine

During the nineteenth century Ireland went through enormous changes. At this time, Ireland was part of the United Kingdom. Under the Poor Laws Act workhouses were built as many Irish people were very poor. When the famine arrived many people died, others were forced to seek refuge in workhouses and many hundreds of thousands left the country.

History Detective

One eyewitness to the famine was Fr Theobald Matthew. In December 1846 he wrote in a letter:

> 'Men, women and children are gradually wasting away. They fill their stomachs with cabbage leaves, turnip tops and the like to appease the cravings of hunger. At this moment, there are more than 5,000 half-starved wretched beings from the country begging in the streets of Cork. When utterly exhausted, they crawl to the workhouse to die.'

1. What in this letter tells you how desperate for food some people were?

2. Why do you think people fled to cities like Cork and Dublin during the famine?

3. What does this letter tell you about how people felt about the workhouses?

The Act of Union – Ireland becomes part of the United Kingdom of Great Britain and Ireland

— 1801

Poor Laws Act – Workhouses established in Ireland

— 1838

The population of Ireland reaches eight million, an increase of almost 50% since 1800

— 1841

The potato crop fails due to blight. Britain responds to the crisis by starting public works and importing food

— 1845

Did You Know?

1847 was the worst year of the famine and was known as Black '47. People died of starvation and of diseases such as typhus and cholera. While people all over the country were dying, many emigrated in search of a better life.

The population has fallen from 8,175,124 people to 6,552,385 from 1841 due to the famine, because of starvation and emigration
1851

The harvest is healthy this year
1850

Queen Victoria visits Ireland
1849

The crops fail again; over one million people are dependent on the Poor Law for relief
1848

Half the population is reliant on soup kitchens and 714,000 people are employed on public works
1847

The potato crop fails again; people die of starvation
1846

Checkpoint

1. When did Ireland become part of the United Kingdom of Great Britain and Ireland?

2. How did the British government respond to the crisis of the potato famine at first?

3. Which British monarch visited Ireland during this period? When did they visit?

4. What effect did the famine have on the population of Ireland?

Emigration During the Famine

During the famine, half a million people died in Ireland of starvation and even more died from disease. Hundreds of thousands of people emigrated to begin a new life in another country. The poorest emigrants travelled to Liverpool and other British ports. These journeys only took a few hours and were far less expensive than voyages to America. Some landlords paid for their tenants to travel to Britain, seeing it as a way to get rid of them cheaply.

▲ Irish emigrants leaving their home for America

People who travelled to Britain knew that food rations awaited them there, far better in quality than what was offered in Ireland. However, conditions for Irish emigrants were far from ideal as many could only afford cheap accommodation in damp and overcrowded buildings.

Thousands more people headed to America. But many of the ships were built to carry cargo not passengers. Life on board was tough and disease spread rapidly. Many people brought no food with them for the journey and depended on the rations handed out. Poor cooking conditions on board meant that food was often undercooked, and often people became sick. So many people died crossing the Atlantic Ocean that the ships became known as 'coffin ships'.

It was expensive to travel to America. Often families could only afford to send one son or daughter to America. That person would then find work there and send money home to help the rest of the family in Ireland. The money that flowed into Ireland also helped families to send more members abroad in search of work and a better life.

▲ Memorial to Emigrants, Boston

Think and Discuss

1. What preparations would a family travelling to America during the famine need to make before leaving, do you think?

2. Why do you think disease spread rapidly on board the coffin ships?

Design and Draw

Design a poster advertising an emigrant ship sailing to America. Include the name of your ship, where it is headed to and leaving from. Use a picture of a real 'coffin ship' if you can.

The Key to Literacy

Research what life was like for Irish emigrants during the famine years once they arrived in America. Imagine you are one of these Irish emigrants. Write a letter to your family describing your voyage across the Atlantic. Talk about why you left and about the advantages and disadvantages of your new life compared to life back in Ireland.

History Detective

Donnelly		John
Family Name		Give Name
alone		
Accompanied by		
50 m	☐ ☐ ☐ ☐	Labourer
Age: Yrs. Mos. Sex	M. S. W. D.	Occupation
Irish	Waterford	Boston
Nationality	Last permanent Residence (TOWN, COUNTRY, ETC.)	Destination
Boston	Sunbeam	14/3/1849
Port of entry	Name of vessel	Date

1. What information can you tell about this person from reading this document?

2. In what year was this person born?

3. What do you think the boxes labelled 'M', 'W', 'S' and 'D' mean?

Long-Term Effects of the Famine

By 1851, the worst of the famine was over, but the effects are still being felt today. The population of Ireland was over eight million people in 1841. However a census taken in 1851, just ten years later, showed the population had decreased by one and a half million. The population continued to fall due to emigration in the years that followed. Emigration became a part of Irish life for generations. In 1850, there were more Irish people living in New York than in Dublin.

Following the famine there was anger at both the British government and the landlords who did little to help the people of Ireland. Irish people had died of starvation, while food was being exported out of the country to places such as Britain. The Irish people began to seek political change.

▲ *Charles Stewart Parnell*

Some people looked for peaceful ways to try to bring about change. Charles Stewart Parnell and Michael Davitt fought for and achieved land reforms, helping tenant farmers. Others decided that only violence would free Ireland from British rule. In 1848, there was an Irish rebellion against British rule.

The rebellion failed, and some of the leaders fled to the United States. There, the leaders raised money for rebel groups that later played an important role in the fight for Irish freedom.

Did You Know?

The Irish language, which was already starting to die out, declined greatly during the famine. This was because many of those who died or emigrated spoke Irish.

Checkpoint

1. What effect did the famine have on the population of Ireland?

2. Why were Irish people angry at the British government and landlords after the famine?

3. What did Charles Stewart Parnell and Michael Davitt do to change the situation?

Lesson Wrap-Up

Visual Summary

The Great Famine was a major event in Irish history. The failure of the potato harvest led to widespread starvation.

Diseases such as typhus killed even more people than starvation. The landlords evicted thousands of tenants who were unable to pay rent from their homes.

Millions of Irish people emigrated to Britain and North America. Today memorials in Ireland and America remember the suffering of those who died or emigrated.

What Did I Learn?

What have I learned in this chapter?

_____

_____

What else would I like to know?

_____

_____

Where can I find this information?

_____

Review

1. **Recall**

   Why was 1847 known as 'Black '47'?

2. **Vocabulary**

   I begin with the 5th letter of the alphabet and I am eight letters long. I am used to describe the action whereby a landlord forces a tenant out of their home.

3. **Critical Thinking**

   Compare what happened during the Irish famine with what happens when there is a famine today. How do modern governments deal with famines?

4. **Be a Historian!**

   Ask your relatives if they know what happened to your ancestors during the Great Famine. Do you have any relations in the United States or Britain as a result of emigration? Do some research then write a report of your findings.

8 The War to End All Wars

What Will I Learn?

- About how the First World War started.
- About the fighting that took place during the war.
- About how the war affected people's lives.
- About the aftermath of the war.

Think and Discuss

1. Describe what you see in each of these pictures.

2. What do you already know about the First World War?

3. Why do you think it was called the First World War? Do you think the whole world was affected by it?

4. Is there any evidence in your local area of wars?

5. In what ways has warfare changed since the First World War?

6. Do you know of any wars happening in the world today?

Key Vocabulary

colonies alliances **allies**

civilians

treaty

assassinated **Armistice Day**

military

The First World War

The Start of the War

Before the war started in 1914, the nations of Europe ruled much of the world. Many European countries such as Britain, Germany and France owned large colonies. To protect their interests, the nations of Europe formed alliances to defend themselves. If one nation was attacked then their allies would go to war to defend that country.

In 1914, Archduke Franz Ferdinand, the heir to the Austro-Hungarian Empire, and his wife Sophie were shot. They were assassinated by a Serb nationalist while in Sarajevo. This event sparked a war in Europe. Austria declared war on Serbia which drew Russia into the war to aid Serbia an ally. Germany declared war on Russia, and on France, as France was a Russian ally. When Germany invaded Belgium to get to France, Britain entered the war to defend Belgium.

▲ The shooting of Archduke Franz Ferdinand

Countries became involved because of old treaties and alliances in which they had agreed in writing to help certain countries if a war situation arose. For example, Britain entered the war to help Belgium because of the terms of a 75-year-old treaty. When Britain got involved, so too did all the countries of the commonwealth, including Australia and Canada. This is how it grew into being a 'world' war because one by one nearly all the countries in the world were affected in some way. When the war began it was first named 'the Great War' as it was believed at the time to be 'the war to end all wars'.

First World War Alliances
- Allied Powers
- Central Powers
- Neutral Nations

Atlantic Ocean

Norway
Sweden
Ireland
Great Britain
Denmark
Netherlands
Belgium
Lux.
Germany
Russia
France
Switz.
Austria-Hungary
Portugal
Spain
Italy
Romania
Montenegro
Serbia
Albania
Bulgaria
Black Sea
Greece
Turkey
The Ottoman Empire
Morocco
Algeria
Tunisia
Mediterranean Sea
Libya
Egypt

Did You Know?

Austria, or Austria-Hungary as it was then known, and its allies were called the Central Powers. The countries fighting against them were called the Allied Powers.

Checkpoint

1. What event sparked the First World War?

2. What drew Britain into the war?

3. Who were the central powers?

During the War

Most of the fighting during the war took place in purpose-dug trenches in mainland Europe. The places where fighting occurred were called the fronts. The Western Front was located between Germany and the part of Belgium that was taken over by Germany and Northern France. The Eastern Front was situated between Germany and Russia. The space between one side's trenches and the other side's trenches, 'the enemy lines', was known as 'No Man's Land'.

Although fighting was only expected to last a short time, it ended up lasting for four years. Many battles were fought, including the Battle of the Somme on the Western Front in Northern France. This was one of the bloodiest battles of the war where many British, Irish, French and German soldiers lost their lives.

▲ *A re-enactment of the Battle of the Somme*

During the four years of the war, developments in military equipment were seen. In 1914, single-seater fighter planes were built. In 1915, the British used poisoned gas for the first time. Other equipment used included armoured tanks, airships, hand grenades, machine guns and shells.

America joined the war in 1917, by which stage the situation had reached a stalemate. Their arrival meant that the allies could launch new attacks on the Western Front. Russia pulled out of the war in 1918. This meant that the German soldiers that had been fighting on the Eastern Front moved to the Western Front to join the fight there.

The fighting continued until the Germans surrendered on 11 November 1918. This day is now known as Armistice Day. Armistice is another word for 'truce'.

After the War

Immediately following the end of the war the people of the affected countries poured onto the streets in celebration. For four years the world had been at war. Many people lost their lives. Estimates suggest that approximately 9 million soldiers and 6 million civilians died. Many of the great empires of Europe had been destroyed and the world looked to establish a lasting peace.

The American President, Woodrow Wilson, proposed a Fourteen Point Peace Plan. In 1919, a peace conference was held. There the Treaty of Versailles was signed. This treaty forced the Germans to pay compensation called reparations to the winning countries. Germany also lost land in Europe, their colonies in Africa and their army was also limited. German anger at the conditions of the treaty would later have effects that would lead to the Second World War.

▲ Allied leaders – Woodrow Wilson, Raymond Poincaré and David Lloyd George

Research and Write It

Research the Treaty of Versailles. Find out who the four main political leaders involved in drafting the Treaty were. What did they want the Treaty to achieve? Now imagine you are a German journalist. Write a newspaper article about the conditions of the agreement for Germany.

▲ Commemoration of the end of the First World War, London, 1919

Did You Know?

Approximately eight million horses died in the First World War.

TIMELINE: FIRST WORLD WAR

1914	1916	1917	1918	1919
War breaks out in Europe	The battle of the Somme	America enters the war	The war ends on 11 November	The Treaty of Versailles is signed

The First World War –
A British Child's Experience

5 July 1916

Dear Diary,

We got news today from Father about the terrible fighting taking place on the Western Front, on the banks of the River Somme in France. Uncle Bernard was injured in the battle but hasn't been sent home yet. Poor Auntie Patricia is very worried and so is Mother. Father sent this picture with his letter.

Uncle Bernard took the picture just before he was hit by a shell in the shoulder. Those poor men, it seems like such an awful place to be. I hope Father will be home soon. It is his birthday in a few weeks – I don't want him to be in such a dreadful place again for his birthday. I heard there were rats the size of cats in those trenches. Still, things aren't too bad for us. Mrs Barry's son was killed in the battle. We will have to pray for the family.

Yours,
Sarah Anne

17 July 1916

Dear Diary,

I'm sick of this war! Mother has to work now and we are left at Grandma's house. I don't like her cooking nearly as much as I like Mother's cooking. Grandma scolds me for complaining so much about the war. She says that all the women have to work now as the men are away and the country needs to keep going. Mother and Auntie Patricia work in an arms factory making weapons. Hundreds of other women work there.

Mother has promised to bring us to the cinema next weekend if we are good for Grandma. She says we all need a good day out! I am really excited about it.

Yours,
Sarah Anne

26 July 1916

Dear Diary,

We haven't heard anything from Father for a while. Mother is getting worried but the other women on the street assure her that we would have heard if something was wrong. Grandma keeps taking us to the allotment to take our minds off it. 'Our plot has the best vegetables around!' she keeps saying. Even still we are always hungry. Before the war we could eat as much bread as we liked, but now we have to make it last for a long time. The flour is needed to make bread to feed all the soldiers, and we can do without it. School will start again soon. I am looking forward to going back. I think it might help us to forget about the war, at least for a few hours a day.

Yours,
Sarah Anne

3 September 1916

Dear Diary,

A letter came from Father today. I'm so upset, as is everyone else here. He is having an awful time in the trenches. He is cold and hungry and tired. He can't sleep anymore. There is constant noise: grenades, shooting, men crying, people having nightmares about the fighting. The worst part is how they die, Mother stopped us from reading most of that page. Uncle Bernard's infection has gotten worse so he should be home by the weekend, Father has to stay though. Father will be so lonely when Uncle Bernard leaves but it will be good for us to see him again, especially for Auntie Patricia. Hopefully Uncle Bernard will tell us more about how Father is.

Yours,
Sarah Anne

Think About It

1. What effect was the war having on Sarah Anne?

2. How was the war affecting Sarah Anne's father?

3. How, do you think, did her father feel during the Battle of the Somme?

4. How, do you think, did her mother feel when she got the letter on 3 September?

The Key to Literacy
Write a diary entry from Sarah Anne on the day she is reunited with her father at the end of the war in 1918.

Lesson Wrap-Up

Visual Summary

The First World War began in 1914 and lasted until 1918. It involved many European nations as well as America, Canada and Australia.

The Battle of the Somme in France was one of the bloodiest battles of the war. It occurred in 1916 on the Western Front.

The war ended on 11 November 1918, a day now known as Armistice Day. In 1919 the Treaty of Versailles was signed, forcing Germany to compensate the winners of the war.

What Did I Learn?

What have I learned in this chapter?

What else would I like to know?

Where can I find this information?

Review

1. **Recall**

   Who were the Central Powers? Who were the Allied Powers?

2. **Vocabulary**

   Explain the term 'allies'. Use it in a sentence about the First World War.

3. **Critical Thinking**

   Read the following stanza of 'Dulce et Decorum Est', a poem by Wilfred Owen about the First World War. What does this stanza reveal about a soldier's experience of the War? Is it a good source of evidence? Why?/Why not?

   'Bent double, like old beggars under sacks,
   Knock-kneed, coughing like hags, we cursed through sludge,
   Till on the haunting flares we turned our backs
   And towards our distant rest began to trudge.
   Men marched asleep. Many had lost their boots
   But limped on, blood-shod. All went lame; all blind;
   Drunk with fatigue; deaf even to the hoots
   Of tired, outstripped Five-Nines that dropped behind.'

4. **Be a Historian!**

   Use the information in this book and information from other sources to create your own detailed timeline of the events of the First World War.

9 Ireland and the Great War

What Will I Learn?

- About Ireland's involvement in the First World War.
- About the lives of some people involved in the war.
- To look at pieces of evidence from the war and take information from them.

"I'll go too!"

THE REAL IRISH SPIRIT

SINN FEIN REBELLION.
HOTEL METROPOLE AND POST OFFICE, DUBLIN
BEFORE AND AFTER.

POBLACHT NA H EIREANN.
THE PROVISIONAL GOVERNMENT
OF THE
IRISH REPUBLIC
TO THE PEOPLE OF IRELAND.

IRISHMEN AND IRISHWOMEN In the name of God and of the dead generations from which she receives her old tradition of nationhood, Ireland, through us, summons her children to her flag and strikes for her freedom.

Having organised and trained her manhood through her secret revolutionary organisation, the Irish Republican Brotherhood, and through her open military organisations, the Irish Volunteers and the Irish Citizen Army, having patiently perfected her discipline, having resolutely waited for the right moment to reveal itself, she now seizes that moment, and, supported by her exiled children in America and by gallant allies in Europe, but relying in the first on her own strength, she strikes in full confidence of victory.

We declare the right of the people of Ireland to the ownership of Ireland, and to the unfettered control of Irish destinies, to be sovereign and indefeasible. The long usurpation of that right by a foreign people and government has not extinguished the right, nor can it ever be extinguished except by the destruction of the Irish people. In every generation the Irish people have asserted their right to national freedom and sovereignty, six times during the past three hundred years they have asserted it in arms. Standing on that fundamental right and again asserting it in arms in the face of the world, we hereby proclaim the Irish Republic as a Sovereign Independent State, and we pledge our lives and the lives of our comrades-in-arms to the cause of its freedom, of its welfare, and of its exaltation among the nations.

The Irish Republic is entitled to, and hereby claims, the allegiance of every Irishman and Irishwoman. The Republic guarantees religious and civil liberty, equal rights and equal opportunities to all its citizens, and declares its resolve to pursue the happiness and prosperity of the whole nation and of all its parts, cherishing all the children of the nation equally, and oblivious of the differences carefully fostered by an alien government, which have divided a minority from the majority in the past.

Until our arms have brought the opportune moment for the establishment of a permanent National Government, representative of the whole people of Ireland and elected by the suffrages of all her men and women, the Provisional Government, hereby constituted, will administer the civil and military affairs of the Republic in trust for the people.

We place the cause of the Irish Republic under the protection of the Most High God, Whose blessing we invoke upon our arms, and we pray that no one who serves that cause will dishonour it by cowardice, inhumanity, or rapine. In this supreme hour the Irish nation must, by its valour and discipline and by the readiness of its children to sacrifice themselves for the common good, prove itself worthy of the august destiny to which it is called.

Signed on Behalf of the Provisional Government,
THOMAS J. CLARKE.
SEAN Mac DIARMADA.   THOMAS MacDONAGH,
P. H. PEARSE,   EAMONN CEANNT,
JAMES CONNOLLY.   JOSEPH PLUNKETT.

AN IRISH
1 IRISHMAN D
10 GERM

SERGEANT MICHAEL
IRISH GU
HAVE YOU NO WISH TO
BRAVERY OF YOUR FE

JOIN AN IRIS
REGIM

1. Describe the three colourful posters.

2. What do you think the aim of the posters is?

3. Who do you think created the posters?

4. Are there any war memorials in your locality?

5. Many Irish soldiers fought in the First World War for the United Kingdom, as Ireland was part of the United Kingdom at the time. Where might these soldiers have fought?

6. Fighting also occurred in Ireland during the war. Why do you think this was?

Key Vocabulary

conscription   enlisted

Home Rule   **victory**

Irish Citizen Army

Rising   **separatist**

Understanding Ireland's Involvement in the War

Hello. My name is Husna and I am a history student. I am researching Ireland's involvement in the First World War. My great-grandfather was from Belfast and fought in the war in the 36th Division. I was fascinated to find out that at the time of the war Ireland was part of the United Kingdom of Great Britain and Ireland. This had been the case since 1801. At the time there was no conscription in Ireland. This meant that people were not forced to fight in the war, yet surprisingly 210,000 Irishmen served in the British forces during the First World War. I was very keen to find out why so many people enlisted. I found this quote from Tom Barry, a man who served in the war.

'In June, in my seventeenth year, I had decided to see what this Great War was like. I cannot plead I went on the advice of John Redmond or any other politician, that if we fought for the British we would secure Home Rule for Ireland, nor can I say I understood what Home Rule meant. I was not influenced by the lurid appeal to fight to save Belgium or small nations. I knew nothing about nations, large or small. I went to the war for no other reason than that I wanted to see what war was like, to get a gun, to see new countries and to feel a grown man.'

I was then very interested to find out who John Redmond was and what Home Rule meant. I used the internet and books in my university's library to find out the answers. I found out that many people in Ireland were unhappy about being ruled from the parliament in Westminster. They wanted their own parliament in Ireland to deal with some issues and the parliament in Westminster to deal with other issues such as foreign affairs. These people were called nationalists and they supported the Home Rule Bill. This bill was due to be passed into law in September 1914 but war broke out in August. Many of the nationalists enlisted to fight, believing that by helping Britain during the war they would be rewarded and the Home Rule Bill would become law. John Redmond was a nationalist leader who encouraged other nationalists to fight for Britain during the war. He encouraged other nationalists to do this also. Here is a cartoon showing John Redmond, leader of the Irish Parliamentary Party who tried to bring about Home Rule.

▲ *John Redmond in Home Rule cartoon*

My great-grandfather was a unionist, meaning he wanted Ireland to remain part of the United Kingdom of Great Britain and Ireland and wanted the parliament to remain in Westminster. When the war broke out, many unionists believed that if they supported Britain in the war then they would be rewarded for their efforts and the Home Rule Bill would not be passed.

People also joined the British forces as the wages were good and it was difficult to find work at the time. If a man joined the army his spouse would also receive money while he was fighting abroad. To many men struggling to find work this seemed like a good opportunity. Other men, like Tom Barry, joined the army for an adventure.

Checkpoint

1. What does the word 'conscription' mean?

2. How many Irishmen served in the British forces during the First World War?

3. Who was John Redmond?

4. According to Husna, what different reasons did men have for fighting during the war?

History Detective

Look at the different sources of information Husna used to find out about the war.

1. What reasons did Tom Barry have for going to war?

2. How do you think the nationalists felt at the outbreak of war?

3. Why did John Redmond encourage people to join the army?

4. Describe the message of the cartoon shown.

Design and Draw

Imagine you are the leader of the Irish Parliamentary Party who wants to see the Home Rule Bill passed into law. Design and draw a poster encouraging nationalists to go to war for Britain.

Research and Write It

Husna's great-grandfather fought with the 36th Division in the war. Other divisions who fought in the First World War include the 10th Irish Division and the 16th Irish Division. Pick one division and research it. Write about that division and their involvement in the war.

Fighting During the War

My family held on to some of the letters, pictures and other documents that link my great-grandfather to the war. Below is a letter he wrote to his wife describing his part in the Battle of Messines which occurred in Belgium in June 1917. I found out through looking up family and church records that my great-grandfather returned safely to Ireland but died some years later, in 1920, during the War of Independence.

8 June 1917

Dearest Sarah,

By now I am sure you have heard the news of our tremendous victory at Messines. The reports suggest that we killed over 10,000 Germans with our explosives. The power of the explosion was felt as far away as Dublin. Many prisoners have been taken as well. This has been one of the most successful battles yet and I sense that we are coming nearer to a final victory over the Germans. Despite our successes we did lose lives. One of the officers was knocked over by the blast and didn't survive. Many others also suffered, some are even missing.

I wanted to tell you for so long about this plan as I was closely involved in its execution. Here is a photograph of us working in the mines on the outskirts of the town planting the explosives. We celebrated last night on French foods and wines – the Catholics and the Protestants together. Maybe after the success of this battle we will learn to work together at home as we did on the battlefield in recent days.

Please tell me, dear, how are you and the children? Have you been able to arrange enough food for the family? I expect that your efforts in the allotment have been fruitful. I must go now, we will be moving on soon but I look forward to your reply. If you can send a package of treats too I would be grateful.

With best love from,
Jeremy

Checkpoint

1. In what year did the Battle of Messines take place?

2. Where was the Battle of Messines?

3. How many Germans died in the attack?

Did You Know?

The Irish who fought in the war suffered heavy losses, particularly in the Battle of the Somme. In the first days of the battle, in July 1916, over 5,500 Irish soldiers died out of a total of around 15,000. Most of these were from the 36th Division. The Twelfth of July Orange Parades were cancelled and a five minute silence was held in Belfast in memory of those who lost their lives.

Date It

The Lusitania was a British liner. During the First World War it was torpedoed off the coast of Cork by a German U-boat. A total of 1,198 people died. Find out when this event happened. Create a timeline of the First World War and add in this date.

Over to You

Carry out a research project about Ireland's involvement in the war. Pick one of the following projects:

- Focus on the lives and experiences of those who fought in the war
- Explore the effect that the war had on those who remained in Ireland
- If you have a relative who fought in the war try to find out about that person
- Choose someone famous who fought in the war and research their life

The War at Home – A Child's Experience

20 April 1916

Dear Diary,

James Connolly was over at our house again last night. Mam and Dad told us to go upstairs. Mr Connolly is the leader of the Irish Citizen Army and that was the second time he and some other men were over. I snuck down to get a glass of water and heard them discussing plans. I heard my father say the words 'England's extremity is Ireland's opportunity'. I wonder what they are planning. Dad hates how the English rule us; he refuses to go to war to fight on their behalf. Even after the posters about the sinking of the Lusitania and some of the neighbours enlisting he still refused. I don't blame him; I don't think it is right either. Maybe I'll ask him about the plans and what he meant by saying 'England's extremity is Ireland's opportunity'. Then he'd know I was listening and I'd get in trouble. I can't ask Mam, she has already given out to me today for taking an extra slice of bread!

Secretly,
Padraig

26 April 1916

Dear Diary,

I knew it! They were planning something all along. Dad is still out there fighting with the others in the ICA. Mam says we took the British completely by surprise. It's perfect – sure, all their attention is focused on the war. They're out there at Liberty Hall, at Jacobs, the GPO, the Four Courts – they are all over the city. I wish I was allowed out, Mam says it's too dangerous though.

Secretly,
Padraig

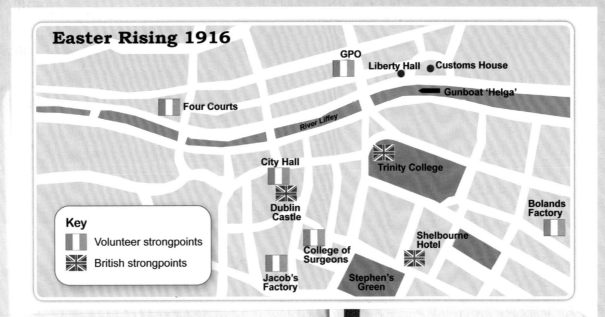

Easter Rising 1916

Map labels:
- GPO
- Liberty Hall
- Customs House
- Gunboat 'Helga'
- Four Courts
- River Liffey
- City Hall
- Trinity College
- Dublin Castle
- Bolands Factory
- College of Surgeons
- Shelbourne Hotel
- Jacob's Factory
- Stephen's Green

Key
- Volunteer strongpoints
- British strongpoints

---

1 May 1916

Dear Diary,

I can't believe that people in Dublin are giving out so much about the Rising. My dad was shot fighting for Ireland's freedom and yet people in the city are giving out about the destruction of buildings. It's not fair. Auntie Mary says that the men who fought are heroes and I agree! If we were our own country then a lot of men wouldn't be fighting over in Europe. Dad says the nationalist soldiers are silly, fighting for Britain and expecting to get Home Rule in return.

Secretly,
Padraig

---

3 July 1916

Dear Diary,

It's so sad to hear the news that so many Irish people have died in France. The newspapers say that about a third of all the Irish people who are over there are dead now because our soldiers were the first to go over the top. I don't know anybody out there but I can imagine how it must feel. I was so upset when Dad got shot during the Rising. We thought he might die for a while. It must be worse though being here with your father over there. Mike from school has an uncle out there but he hasn't heard anything yet. This war was supposed to be over before Christmas, and that was two years ago! Hopefully the fighting will end soon.

Secretly,
Padraig

Think About It

1. Why do you think a Rising was held in Ireland during the war?

2. What, do you think, did those involved in the Rising want to achieve?

3. Many of those responsible for the Rising were executed. What effect do you think this had on the people of Dublin?

4. How do you think Padraig's view of the war differed from that of other Irish children?

Did You Know?

The execution of James Connolly had a huge effect on the people of Dublin, who didn't support the Rising at the time. It changed many of their opinions and fuelled support for the republican separatist movement. Connolly Station in Dublin city centre and Connolly Hospital in Blanchardstown are both named after James Connolly.

The Key to Literacy

Writing

Research the life of James Connolly, the leader of the Irish Citizen Army who was executed by firing squad for his role in the Easter Rising. Write a short biography about his life. Remember, a biography is an account of someone's life.

▲ Kilmainham Gaol

Over to You

This is a picture of the Irish National War Memorial Gardens. A memorial is something that reminds us of a person or event. This memorial commemorates the 49,000 Irish people who died during the First World War. Find out if there are any war memorials in your area and what they commemorate.

Visual Summary

Ireland was part of United Kingdom during the First World War. In all, about 210,000 Irish soldiers fought in the war.

Nationalists went to war because they thought Home Rule would then be granted. Unionists went because they thought it would mean Home Rule would not be granted.

While many didn't initially support the 1916 Rising, the execution of the rebels turned public opinion against the British.

What Did I Learn?

What have I learned in this chapter?

What else would I like to know?

Where can I find this information?

Review

1. **Recall**

   What reasons did Irishmen have for going to war?

2. **Vocabulary**

   Write a list of words that mean the same as 'enlisted'.

3. **Critical Thinking**

   After the execution of the leaders of the Easter Rising, public opinion turned and many people no longer wanted to be ruled by Britain. What effect do you think this had on the soldiers who fought for Britain during the war?

4. **Be a Historian!**

   Select one primary source from the chapter e.g. a poster or cartoon, and write down three things it tells you about the time.

10 Young History Makers

What Will I Learn?

- About the lives of three people who played a role in history.
- To describe the actions and feelings of these people as they made history.
- To describe the attitudes and motivations of these people.

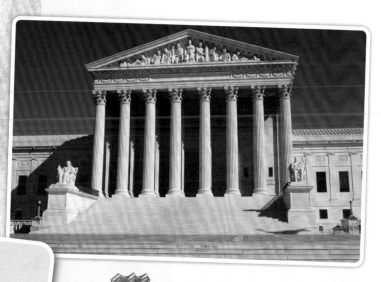

Think and Discuss

1. Describe what you see in each of these pictures.

2. Where are the objects and buildings shown in the pictures located, do you think?

3. Do you recognise any of the people in the pictures? If so, what do you already know about them?

4. Which is your favourite picture and why?

Key Vocabulary

Tutankhamun

segregation

pharaoh

Irish Volunteers

court martial

comrades   heretic

War of Independence

King Tutankhamun
– The Boy Pharaoh from Egypt

Tutankhamun is probably the most famous Egyptian pharaoh. Historians believe he began ruling the eighteenth dynasty of the Egyptian Empire when he was nine years old. Because he was a young ruler, historians believe real decision making would have been done by senior army officials. British archaeologist Howard Carter discovered Tutankhamun's tomb in 1922, nearly 3,000 years after his death.

Tutankhamun's father, Akhenaten, was declared a heretic because he introduced a new religion. Egyptian officials destroyed all records of Akhenaten and his successors. For that reason, historians know relatively little about Tutankhamun. It is known, however, that he married his half-sister and had no surviving children.

▲ Howard Carter (on left) at the entrance to the tomb, 1922

▲ Tomb of Tutankhamun, Valley of the Kings, Egypt

It is believed that he died at the age of 18, though the exact cause of his death is unknown. Egyptologists found bone fragments inside his skull, which could have been caused by a blow to the head or an accident such as a fall. For a long time, many speculated that the boy ruler was murdered. More recently, evidence has indicated that Tutankhamun died as a result of complications with a broken leg.

Tutankhamun is most famous for the treasures which were discovered in his tomb in the Valley of the Kings. Ancient Egyptians believed that he would remain a pharaoh after his death and would therefore need to take his worldly possessions with him. They filled his tomb with chariots, thrones, furniture, food and jewellery – there were so many items it took archaeologists 10 years to carefully remove everything. Tutankhamun was mummified and found wearing a death mask of gold and coloured glass. His tomb was decorated with several paintings.

Tutankhamun's treasures were put on display in the Egyptian Museum in Cairo, Egypt. Museums around the world have exhibited replica treasures so that everyone can appreciate the elaborate tomb in which he was buried.

Think and Discuss

1. How, do you think, did Tutankhamun feel about becoming pharaoh at such a young age?

2. How do you think the people ruled by Tutankhamun felt about him?

3. What does the burial of Tutankhamun tell you about the beliefs of ancient Egyptians?

4. What, do you think, was the purpose of the Egyptian death mask?

Did You Know?

Some people who excavated Tutankhamun's tomb met an early death. Many newspapers claimed they had unleashed a curse said to have been written in hieroglyphics in the tomb. The curse translated means 'Death Shall Come on Swift Wings to Him Who Disturbs the Peace of the King'.

Over to You

It was very important to the ancient Egyptians that human bodies be preserved after death. They used a process called mummification to do this. Research mummification and draw a diagram that explains what happens during this process.

TIMELINE: TUTANKHAMUN

1346 BC	1337 BC	1328 BC	AD 1922
Tutankhamun is born in Akhetaten, the capital city of Egypt at the time	Tutankhamun becomes the pharaoh of the Egyptian Empire	Tutankhamun dies around the age of 18	British archaeologists discover Tutankhamun's tomb in the Valley of the Kings

Linda Brown
– The Kansas Girl Who Took on the Board of Education

▲ Monroe Elementary School, now the 'Brown vs. Board of Education National Historic Site'

In 1951, Linda Brown was seven years old and living in Topeka, Kansas. Every day, she walked over one and a half kilometres to the bus stop to get a bus to school. Although there was an elementary school very close to her home, she was not allowed to attend because of her colour.

Linda was African American and the school around the corner was a 'white elementary school' – only white children could attend.

When Linda was growing up, there was much segregation; white and black people belonged to separate clubs and sports teams. Black people were not allowed to eat in the same restaurants or drink from the same water fountains. Of the 22 elementary schools in the Topeka area, four were for black students only. The 'black schools' were underfunded, overcrowded and lacked supplies such as textbooks.

Linda's father, Rev. Oliver Brown, decided to work with the NAACP (National Association for the Advancement of Coloured People) to help solve the issue. Together they took a case against the Topeka education board's segregation of schools, which became known as *Brown vs. Board of Education*.

Did You Know?
The school for black children that Linda got a bus to was called the Monroe Elementary School. The school is now the 'Brown vs. Board of Education National Historic Site'.

▲ A formerly segregated water fountain in Monroe Elementary School

▲ Segregation in Monroe Elementary School

The NAACP hired lawyers and challenged the state to change the laws so that black children could attend the same schools as white children. The NAACP lost their case and the state argued that by treating the children differently, they were better preparing them for a future of unequal treatment.

The NAACP refused to give up and brought their case before the Supreme Court on 1 October 1951. There were several similar cases taking place in America around the same time. All the cases joined together to be fought as one large case on 9 December 1952. Linda's father said that there needed to be proof that black children were different from white children, if they were to continue being treated differently.

The case ended on 17 May 1954 and the court found in favour of Linda Brown and the other black children.

Checkpoint

1. Why did Linda Brown have to walk so far every day?

2. Give three examples of the ways in which white and black people were segregated from each other when Linda was growing up.

3. What was the NAACP?

4. What did the education board need to prove if they were to continue segregating children?

The Key to Literacy

Imagine you are Linda Brown at eight or nine years of age. Write a diary entry about your father's case and say how you feel about the school system.

Think and Discuss

1. How do you think Linda Brown felt when she was walking to the bus stop each day? What might she have been thinking? How would you have felt in a similar situation? Discuss.

2. How do you think Linda Brown felt when the trial was taking place?

3. How do you think Rev. Oliver Brown and the NAACP felt when they won the case?

TIMELINE

Summer 1950		1951	1 October 1951	9 December 1952	17 May 1954
Rev. Oliver Brown tries to enrol his daughter Linda in a local 'white school'. Thirteen other black families try to enrol their children. All are refused because of their race	The parents file a lawsuit against the Topeka Board of Education for their children	The parents lose the case in the state courts and decide to take the case to the US Supreme Courts	Supreme Court hears the appeal	Supreme Court hears from the lawyers	Case ends with the court finding in favour of Linda Brown and the other children

Kevin Barry

– The Irish Boy Who Stood His Ground

Kevin Barry was born in Dublin on 20 January 1902. His family moved to Carlow in 1908. When he was 14, Kevin returned to Dublin. He became interested in politics and joined a battalion of Irish Volunteers in 1916.

Many Irishmen fought for the British army in the First World War. After the First World War ended, many people wanted freedom from British rule and were prepared to fight in order to get it. Some Irish politicians wanted to have their own parliament. This led to the beginning of the War of Independence.

In 1919 Kevin enrolled at Belvedere College to study medicine. He also took part in many arms raids and the burning of an RIC Barracks. By 1920, violent conflicts were taking place between British police and Irish volunteers. That year, on 20 September, Kevin took part in an arms raid in which three British soldiers were killed. Kevin was unable to escape with his comrades. He was found hiding under a lorry and sent to Mountjoy Prison.

▲ Kevin Barry Monument, Rathvilly, County Carlow

Kevin attended a court martial and was charged with killing a soldier. He insisted his actions were acts of war because he was a soldier. During the trial, Kevin showed contempt for the court by reading a newspaper, surprising many people with his brave attitude. Although he had been tortured by the British military, he refused to give the names of his comrades.

After seven days, he was told he would be executed. Kevin did not want to be hanged because he believed that kind of a death was not appropriate for a soldier. He asked to be killed instead by a firing squad.

On 1 November 1920, at 18 years of age, Kevin Barry was hanged in Mountjoy Prison. The execution of such a young Irish man led to mass outrage. Large numbers of volunteers began joining the Irish fight in the War of Independence in part because of what happened to Kevin Barry.

History Detective

Read this excerpt from the song *Kevin Barry*, written after his death.

> Just before he faced the hangman,
> In his dreary prison cell,
> The Black and Tans tortured Barry,
> Just because he wouldn't tell.
> The names of his brave comrades,
> And other things, they wished to know.
> 'Turn informer and we'll free you'
> Kevin Barry answered, 'No'.
>
> Shoot me like a soldier.
> Do not hang me like a dog,
> For I fought to free old Ireland
> On that still September morn.
> 'All around the little bakery
> Where we fought them hand to hand,
> Shoot me like a brave soldier,
> For I fought for Ireland.

1. What does this song suggest about the character of Kevin Barry?

2. How do you think the songwriter felt about Kevin Barry? Why?

Lesson Wrap-Up

Visual Summary

Tutankhamun ruled the Egyptian Empire as a young boy. His tomb was discovered 3,000 years after his death by British archaeologist Howard Carter.

Linda Brown's father, Rev. Oliver Brown, took a case to the Supreme Court which brought an end to segregation in schools.

Kevin Barry was hanged in Mountjoy Prison for the shooting of a British soldier during an arms raid when he was 18 years old.

Review

1. **Recall**

   Who discovered the tomb of Tutankhamun and in what year?

2. **Vocabulary**

   How many syllables are in each of the following words: mummified, Egyptian, segregation, execution, Egyptologist.

3. **Critical Thinking**

   How do you think schooling in America has changed since Linda Brown attended school in the 1950s? Explain at least three ways.

4. **Be a Historian!**

   Find and read the full version of the song Kevin Barry and evaluate whether it is a good source of historical evidence.

What Did I Learn?

What have I learned in this chapter?

What else would I like to know?

Where can I find this information?

What Will I Learn?

- About the origins of conflict in Northern Ireland.
- About the period known as 'The Troubles' in Northern Ireland.
- About the attitudes and beliefs of different groups of people living in Northern Ireland.
- How peace was restored to the region in recent times.

United Kingdom (Northern Ireland)

Galway

Limeri

Clonmel

Waterford

1. Look at the pictures. What do they tell you about the history of Northern Ireland?

2. Why do you think the group of men are marching?

3. How do you feel about the image of the young girl and the soldier?

4. Look at the painting on the side of the house. This is called a mural. What do you think it means?

5. Look at the sculpture of the men reaching out to each other. What do you think it means?

TIME FOR PEACE

TIME TO GO

Key Vocabulary

plantation   unionists

partition   **republicans**

paramilitary

Good Friday Agreement

power-sharing   loyalists

From Early Invaders to the Partition of Ireland

The origins of the battle for ownership of land in Ireland are found in the twelfth century. During this century, an Irish king called Diarmuid MacMurrough needed help to defend himself against a rival king. He invited a group of Normans from England to help him do this. The Normans arrived in Ireland in 1169 and helped Diarmuid MacMurrough to regain the Kingdom of Leinster. In return for their services the Normans were given land. They built many castles and fortresses around the country – some of these can still be seen today. In 1171, the King of England came to Ireland to establish his authority over the Normans. The English king began to seize land around the country for himself.

▲ A Norman castle in Northern Ireland

Did You Know?

Before the arrival of the Normans in Ireland, Ireland was ruled by a succession of High Kings. The High Kings ruled from the Hill of Tara, which was the most important site in Ireland before any of our cities or towns were built.

In the 1500s the English government began a policy in Ireland known as 'plantation'. The native Irish were driven from their land. The confiscated land was then given to English settlers. During the Plantation of Ulster in the early 1600s, land was confiscated from Catholics and given to Protestant settlers from England and Scotland. The native Catholic Irish began to rebel against English rule in Ireland. A highly ranked English soldier, Oliver Cromwell, arrived in 1649 to fight the rebellious Irish. He had an army of 12,000 troops behind him. These men were the best trained and best organised army in Europe.

The Irish were no match. Cromwell was infamously ruthless, and a violent period of history followed his arrival in Ireland. By the end of the war in 1652, almost one-third of the Catholics in Ireland had died as a result of Cromwell's violent campaign to assert English power in Ireland. Many more had been forced off their lands, and a new class of wealthy Protestant landowners was formed.

▲ Oliver Cromwell

▲ William of Orange

The Battle of the Boyne in 1690 led to a historic defeat of the Catholic Irish. During this fierce battle, the Protestant William of Orange defeated the Catholic King James II. The Penal Laws were introduced to try and prevent Catholics from rising up again. Catholics were discriminated against because of these laws, which remained in place for over a hundred years. The Penal Laws prevented Catholics from voting, owning land or holding powerful positions in society. The Act of Union in 1801 led to the closure of the Irish parliament. Ireland was now directly controlled by the British government. In the 1870s, the Home Rule League was established. Its leader, Charles Stewart Parnell, fought for Ireland's right to set up its own government in Dublin.

Checkpoint

1. When did the Normans come to Ireland?

2. What was the Plantation of Ulster and when did it happen?

3. When did Oliver Cromwell come to Ireland?

4. Who was defeated at the Battle of the Boyne?

▲ Charles Stewart Parnell

The Key to Literacy

Use the internet and the library to research the Battle of the Boyne, one of the most famous and fiercest battles in Irish history. Find out who fought at this battle and why. What was the significance of this battle? Imagine you are an onlooker at the scene. Write a poem describing the battle.

Not everyone in Ireland supported the Home Rule movement. Northern unionists, who were mostly Protestant, were against Home Rule. They wanted to stay in union with Britain. In 1912 they formed the Ulster Volunteers to fight for their cause. This group later became the Ulster Volunteer Force (UVF). Irish Nationalists, who were mostly Catholic, supported Home Rule. In 1913, they formed a military group called the Irish Volunteers to fight for Irish independence.

After the 1916 Rising and the Irish War of Independence, Irish and British politicians signed the Anglo-Irish Treaty in 1921. This treaty introduced the partition of Ireland. The 26 counties of southern Ireland would be given their own government and named a Free State. The six counties in the North would remain under British rule.

Checkpoint

1. Who were the UVF and when were they formed?

2. Who were the Irish Volunteers and when were they formed?

3. What was the Anglo-Irish Treaty?

Over to You

Draw a map of Ireland. Colour and name the six counties that remained under British rule following the Anglo-Irish Treaty in 1921.

History Detective

The partition of Ireland into North and South happened in 1921 with the Anglo-Irish Treaty. Ireland is one of many countries that has been divided or partitioned in the course of its history. Some countries that have been partitioned are then reunified later on. Can you find examples of other countries that have been divided and/or reunified? When did this happen? Can you find those countries on a map?

TIMELINE

1169	The Normans arrive in Ireland
King Henry II comes to Ireland	1171
1556	First plantation starts in Ireland
The Plantation of Ulster begins	1606
1649	Oliver Cromwell comes to Ireland
The Battle of the Boyne	1690
1801	Act of Union
Home Rule League is founded	1873
1916	Easter Rising in Dublin
War of Independence begins	1919
1921	Anglo-Irish Treaty signed

'The Troubles' in Northern Ireland

The period known as 'the Troubles' in Northern Ireland began almost 50 years after partition, in the late 1960s. The people living in Northern Ireland were made up of two rival groups. The unionists or loyalists, who were mostly Protestant, were loyal to British politics and its monarchy. They wanted to remain in the United Kingdom. The nationalists or republicans were mostly Catholic. They wanted to be reunited with the South to form a 32-county Republic. They believed that the entire island of Ireland should be free from British rule. The Republicans were represented by their own political party, Sinn Féin.

During the Troubles, paramilitary groups carried out acts of violence and political terrorism on behalf of both groups. On the republican side, the Irish Republican Army (IRA) and the Irish National Liberation Army (INLA) were the main paramilitary groups. The Ulster Volunteer Force and Ulster Defence Association (UDA) were the main paramilitary groups operated by the loyalists. Around 3,000 people died as a result of the fighting between these two rival sides during the Troubles.

Barriers called peacelines were built to separate Catholic and Protestant areas and divided Belfast. Some of these barriers were over six metres high. Murals were painted on houses in both areas to show the views of the people living there. Protestant areas often have murals of William of Orange, known as 'King Billy'.

Catholic areas have murals showing a united Ireland, or imagery showing ancient Irish myths and legends.

During the Troubles, paramilitary groups frequently bombed busy city streets and other public places across Ireland and Britain. Many innocent people were killed in shocking events such as Bloody Sunday and the Omagh bombing.

Checkpoint

1. When did the Troubles begin in Northern Ireland?

2. What were the names of the main paramilitary groups?

3. What is a mural? Why did people paint murals in Belfast?

Did You Know?

The violence in Northern Ireland reached its highest point on 30 January 1972. On that date British soldiers shot and killed 14 people at a banned march. The violence quickly got worse and the British governement declared Direct Rule over Northern Ieland.

Think About It

Peacelines were barriers that separated Catholics from Protestants in Northern Ireland. These barriers still exist today in parts of Belfast. What do you think it would be like if your town/village had barriers to separate people from each other? Do you know of any other cities or countries in the world that use barriers to divide people from each other?

Research and Write It

Look on the internet to find some examples of murals that represent the views of the different people living in Northern Ireland during the Troubles. Choose two murals and describe what you think the artists are trying to say with their images. Try and think from the point of view of the person painting the mural – taking into account their religion, their political views, their age, their hopes and dreams for the future.

The Long Road to Peace

After the partition of Ireland there were many decades of political unrest in Northern Ireland. The effects of the unrest were felt in the south of Ireland and also in Britain. By 1972, Britain and Ireland were desperate to stop the violence. Each year, hundreds of people were dying.

There were many attempts to get the different groups in Northern Ireland working together. However, none of these early attempts were successful. Britain realised that it needed to work with the Republic of Ireland to try to resolve the situation in Northern Ireland. In 1985 the Anglo-Irish Agreement was signed. This agreement would see the Republic of Ireland working with Britain to try to find a solution for the problem in the North.

▲ *John Major and Albert Reynolds, 1994*

In 1994 negotiations between the Taoiseach Albert Reynolds and the British Prime Minister John Major led to the first IRA ceasefire. This meant that the IRA agreed to stop using violent methods to achieve their aims. The UVF also declared a ceasefire shortly afterwards. This marked the first step in the long path to restore peace to Northern Ireland.

Many world leaders became involved in the peace process.

The US President Bill Clinton visited Belfast in 1995 to show his support for peace. The British Prime Minister Tony Blair also took action by agreeing to meet with the Irish nationalist leader Gerry Adams. Mo Mowlam was another British politician who played an active role in peace negotiations. She was successful in arranging multi-party talks and for restoring the IRA ceasefire.

▲ *Dr Mo Mowlam, Secretary of State for Northern Ireland, 1998*

▲ *Bill Clinton*

The Good Friday Agreement

In 1998 Taoiseach Bertie Ahern and British Prime Minister Tony Blair led their two governments to sign the Good Friday Agreement. The agreement promoted partnership, equality and respect between communities in Northern Ireland. Two of the people who were involved in the Good Friday Agreement, John Hume, a Catholic, and David Trimble, a Protestant, received the 1998 Nobel Peace Prize.

▲ John Hume

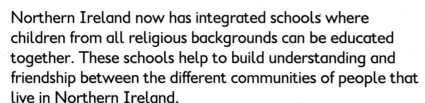

▲ David Trimble

In the years following the Good Friday Agreement, the military groups on both sides began to gradually disarm. This meant that both sides reduced their force and weapons. Today in Northern Ireland, unionists and republicans sit side-by-side in a power-sharing government where each has equal power. This government is called the Northern Ireland Assembly. Its offices are located at Stormont in Belfast.

▲ Stormont

Northern Ireland now has integrated schools where children from all religious backgrounds can be educated together. These schools help to build understanding and friendship between the different communities of people that live in Northern Ireland.

History Detective

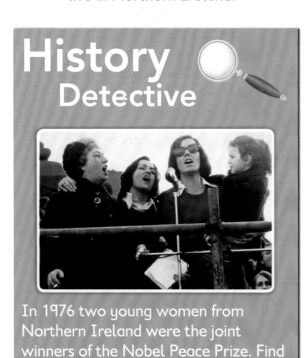

In 1976 two young women from Northern Ireland were the joint winners of the Nobel Peace Prize. Find out more about these two women and the organisation that they established, the Community of Peace People.

Checkpoint

1. What was the Anglo-Irish Agreement?

2. When was the Good Friday Agreement signed?

3. Who received the Nobel Peace Prize in 1998?

4. Where is the Northern Ireland Assembly located?

Over to You

Do you think integrated schools are a good idea? Why? What other kinds of integration do you think would be helpful to achieve better understanding between the different groups of people living in Northern Ireland?

Lesson Wrap-Up

From Conflict to Peace

Mullingar

Carlow

Kil...

Clonmel

Wa...

1. **Recall**

   What was the Good Friday Agreement and when was it signed?

2. **Vocabulary**

   If you didn't know what the word 'paramilitary' meant, how could you find out its meaning? Try to think of at least three different ways.

3. **Critical Thinking**

   The history of Northern Ireland shows that it is possible to achieve peace even between people with opposite points of view. What do you think are the benefits of having a society made up of people with different points of view? What would society be like if everybody had the same viewpoint on everything?

4. **Be a Historian!**

   Create a timeline showing the journey from conflict to peace in Northern Ireland. Use the information in this chapter and information from other sources to help you.

12 Stories from World Changing Women

What Will I Learn?

- About female leaders from the past.
- About the life of Eleanor Roosevelt, human rights campaigner.
- About the life of Mary Robinson, former President of Ireland.
- About the life of Golda Meir, former Prime Minister of Israel.

Blog

Hi, my name is Lisa. I am a professor at Trinity College in Dublin. I study the lives of women from history. Many films show famous queens such as Cleopatra. I am interested in women who are not so famous but made a big difference to the world around them. Some were scientists, others were religious leaders, artists or people who fought to make life better for others. I hope you enjoy reading about some of them.

1. Describe what you see in each of these photos.

2. How do you think the different images of the women were created?

3. What period in history do you think each woman lived or lives in? Are there any clues about what country they come from?

4. What title or job do you think these women had or have?

5. Why do you think there are more female leaders today than in the past?

Key Vocabulary

charity campaign **Zionist**
senator peace process
Áras an Uachtaráin
Seanad Éireann refugees

Eleanor Roosevelt

▲ Eleanor as a child

Eleanor Roosevelt was one of the most important American women of the twentieth century. She was born in New York city on 11 October 1884. Her mother died when she was just eight years old, and her father was an alcoholic. Eleanor and her two brothers went to live with their grandmother.

▲ Franklin D. Roosevelt

Young Eleanor was shy. But at 15 she went to a new school near London, England. Here the headmistress encouraged Eleanor to think for herself and to help other people.

In March 1905, Eleanor married her cousin, Franklin D. Roosevelt. For the next 10 years, she helped him with his political career and had six children. Eleanor also worked for the Red Cross, a medical charity, during the First World War.

▲ Eleanor on a Second World War goodwill tour in Britain

In 1921, Eleanor's husband Franklin lost the use of his legs due to a disease. Eleanor encouraged him to return to politics. She also became famous herself, speaking out for women's and workers' rights.

In 1932, Franklin Roosevelt became the US President. In her role as 'first lady', the wife of the president, Eleanor gave radio broadcasts and travelled around the country. She became known as the 'legs and ears' of her husband. At this time, many Americans had lost their jobs. Eleanor became a voice for people in need.

▲ Eleanor Roosevelt 1933

After the United States joined the Second World War in 1941, Eleanor made regular trips to visit wounded troops. Her husband Franklin Roosevelt died shortly before the end of the war.

Checkpoint

1. Where was Eleanor Roosevelt born?

2. What is the Red Cross?

3. Name three things Eleanor did as 'first lady'.

The new president, Harry S. Truman, gave Eleanor a job working for human rights with the United Nations.

During the last 10 years of her life, Eleanor Roosevelt travelled all over the world. She even visited the Soviet Union, which was America's enemy at that time. Eleanor Roosevelt died on 7 November 1962. She inspired millions with her determination to help other people.

▲ *Eleanor and the United Nations Universal Declaration of Human Rights*

Think About It

1. What do you think it was like for Eleanor growing up in her grandmother's care?

2. Why do you think she was known as the 'ears and legs' of her husband?

3. List three big turning points in Eleanor's life. Give reasons why they were important.

4. What sort of person do you think Eleanor was?

Research and Write It

One of Eleanor Roosevelt's most famous slogans was 'equal pay for equal work'. Research Eleanor's involvement in trade unions for working women. Then imagine you are working with Eleanor to improve life for working women in the 1920s. Think of a good slogan of your own and list three reasons why people should support your campaign.

Mary Robinson

Mary Robinson is a world-famous campaigner who has worked hard to stand up to what she sees as unfair.

She was born Mary Bourke on 21 May 1944 in Ballina in County Mayo. Mary went to Mount Anville school in Dublin and then studied law at Trinity College, Dublin. At 25 she became the youngest ever professor of law in Trinity. She met Nicholas Robinson at the college and married him in 1970.

In 1969, Mary became a senator in the upper house in the Irish Parliament, Seanad Éireann. She remained a senator until 1989. The year after, she became Ireland's first woman president and the youngest ever, aged 46.

Mary was a very popular president. She did a lot to improve Ireland's image overseas. After Mary visited the

▲ Flag of the United Nations

African country of Rwanda she gave a very emotional speech. It shed light on the bloody civil war that had happened there. Mary also helped the peace process in Northern Ireland by meeting rival leaders Gerry Adams and David Trimble.

In 1997, Mary became head of the United Nations Commission (department) for Human Rights. In that role she promoted human rights around the world. She played a role in protecting thousands of refugees in Kosovo in Eastern Europe who had been forced from their homes.

Since 2002, Mary has worked with many other human rights organisations. In 2007, she met with Nelson Mandela and other world leaders to form 'The Elders'. This organisation aims to tackle some of the world's toughest problems.

Date It

Create a timeline for the life of Mary Robinson. Include important milestones in her life such as her marriage, becoming the president of Ireland, and becoming the head of the United Nations Commission for Human Rights.

Did You Know?

Mary Robinson started the tradition of having a lighted candle in the window at Áras an Uachtaráin in Dublin, the official home of the Irish president. It was a symbol to Irish emigrants all over the world that while they might be gone, they were not forgotten.

Her work has led to many international awards, including the US Presidential Medal of Freedom awarded by Barack Obama in 2009.

In recent years, Mary returned to live in Ireland. She currently serves as President of the Mary Robinson Foundation as well as holding other important posts such as Chancellor of the University of Dublin, Trinity College.

▲ *Trinity College, Dublin*

Think About It

1. How do you think Mary's background in law helped her during her career?

2. What qualities helped Mary to be so successful in her career and goals, do you think?

3. Why is it important that Ireland has a good reputation in other countries, do you think?

4. How would you improve human rights around the world?

Research and Write It

Find out about Mary McAleese, Ireland's president after Mary Robinson. Write a brief summary of her life.

Design and Draw

Imagine it is time to elect a new Irish president. Write out a list of all the qualities that the new president needs to have. What kind of experience should the right candidate have? Now you are going to design an election poster for an imaginary presidential candidate. Draw a picture of this candidate on the poster and list their presidential qualities beside it.

The Key to Literacy

Imagine you are a journalist and you are going to get the opportunity to interview Mary Robinson about her life. Write a list of ten questions that you would like to ask her. Remember, you want to get lots of information from Mary Robinson and will therefore need to ask good questions.

Golda Meir

In 1969, Golda Meir became one of the first women in modern times to become a Prime Minister.

Originally named Goldie Mabovitz, she was born in Kiev, formerly part of Russia, on 3 May 1898. When Golda was eight, her family moved to the United States, to escape attacks on Jewish people in Russia. In 1917, she married Morris Myerson. Four years later they went to work on a farm in Palestine and eventually moved to Jerusalem.

Golda also became a member of the Zionist movement. At the time, the British ruled Palestine. The Zionists wanted to set up a new Jewish state called 'Israel' in Palestine, against the wishes of the Arab people living there. This was because Zionists believed that Palestine was the ancient home of the Jewish people and their religion.

In the late 1930s, Golda helped to smuggle Jewish refugees into Palestine who were fleeing from the Nazis in Germany. After the Second World War, the state of Israel was formed. Golda became a minister in the Israeli parliament. She came up with a plan to build thousands of houses and apartments for Jewish refugees. In 1956, Golda was made foreign minister. She changed her surname to Meir, the Hebrew version of Myerson.

In 1969 the Prime Minister of Israel died. Golda agreed to take over, even though she was now 71. As leader, Golda tried to achieve peace in the Middle East. But after an Arab attack caught her country by surprise in 1973, she resigned. Golda died in Jerusalem on 8 December 1978. When she died it was revealed that she had had leukemia for 12 years.

Did You Know?

Golda Meir won many awards in her lifetime. In 1975, Meir was awarded the Israel Prize for her special contribution to society and the state of Israel.

Think and Discuss

1. Why is Golda admired by many people around the world, do you think?

2. How important was being Jewish to Golda, do you think? Explain your answer.

Date It

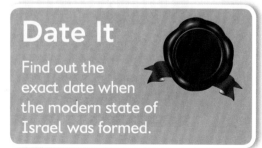

Find out the exact date when the modern state of Israel was formed.

Visual Summary

Eleanor Roosevelt campaigned for workers' and human rights for many years in the United States. She also helped to write the Universal Declaration of Human Rights.

The former Irish President, Mary Robinson, is a world-famous campaigner for human rights.

In 1969, Golda Meir became one of the first women in modern times to become a Prime Minister.

What Did I Learn?

What have I learned in this chapter?

_____

_____

What else would I like to know?

_____

_____

Where can I find this information?

_____

Review

1. **Recall**

   Who inspired Eleanor Roosevelt to help others when she was a teenager?

2. **Vocabulary**

   What does the word 'charity' mean to you? Draw a picture that sums up the word for you.

3. **Critical Thinking**

   In Ireland, and in many other countries, if a person wants to be elected the President they have to be 35 years of age or older. Why do you think this is? Do you think it is a good idea? Why?/Why not?

4. **Be a Historian!**

   Were any famous women born in your local area? Or can you discover any important achievements by a woman from your local area that people don't know about? Choose one such important or famous woman, research her life and and write a short biography.

What Will I Learn?

- How the daily lives of Irish people have changed since the 1950s.
- About emigration and immigration.
- How the population of Ireland has changed since the 1950s.
- About Irish communities living abroad.
- About immigrants living in Ireland today.

Think and Discuss

1. Look at the pictures. The black and white photos were taken in the 1950s. In what ways do you think Ireland has changed since then?

2. Why do you think the men are standing around talking? What does this picture tell us about life in Ireland in those days?

3. Look at the picture of the marketplace. Where do you think it was taken? Give a reason for your answer.

4. What kind of shop is shown in the picture? Do you think there were shops like this in Ireland in the 1950s?

Key Vocabulary

armed forces

economic

downturn

population

unemployment

immigration

recession

prosperity

graduates

The 1950s – The Post-War Era

Ireland has undergone enormous changes since the 1950s. Almost every aspect of daily life has changed.

One of the features of daily life that has remained with us since the 1950s is emigration. In this chapter we will look at some of the reasons why people emigrate and the effect that has on society. We will also look at immigration and how that has changed Irish society in the past two decades.

During the 1930s and 1940s, many Irish people worked in agriculture and local industry, producing goods and services for sale in local markets. Many other Irish people had been employed by the armed forces of Britain and Ireland during the Second World War (1939–1945). When the war ended, there were not enough jobs for everyone. This meant that Ireland faced a number of social and economic challenges in the 1950s.

Ireland had not yet started to trade widely with foreign countries or attract foreign companies, as other countries had. When foreign companies set up they bring jobs and Ireland badly needed jobs for its citizens. At that stage, Ireland was relying on its own home market to provide jobs and keep the economy going. Unemployment levels began to rise in Ireland while other countries were becoming better off as they were trading with each other.

Did You Know?

Economics relates to the financial affairs of countries and the production and consumption of goods and services.

Emigration once again became the only option for many thousands of young people. They began to leave Ireland in search of a better future in countries like the United Kingdom, Canada, and the east coast of America. In the 1950s it is estimated that 400,000 Irish people left for foreign shores.

Seán Lemass, who is known as 'the father of modern Ireland', became Taoiseach in 1959. Lemass began to encourage Ireland to trade with other countries to build up an export business. He also encouraged foreign companies to locate in Ireland. This resulted in the creation of new factories and jobs. Unemployment figures began to fall.

Seán Lemass

Blog

Hi, my name is Kevin O'Brien. I'm the captain of the Liverpool under-18s Gaelic football team. My grandad Rory is our coach. This year we're hoping to make the All-Britain final, which is played at Páirc na hÉireann in Birmingham next October. Grandad says if we make it to the final it will be the first time an O'Brien has played in a GAA final since his dad, my great-grandfather Donal O'Brien. Donal was a champion hurler! He moved from Co. Kerry to Liverpool in the 1950s. There was no work in Ireland back then. He found a job working on construction sites, but he never lost the love of Gaelic games. He met my great-grandmother Maureen at a céilí in Liverpool – she was from Kerry too. Maureen and her two sisters left Ireland to work as nurses over here. They never went back to Ireland. There are 22 O'Brien cousins in total – we all have Irish names. Every summer we go 'home' to Kerry to visit our relatives there. Ireland is a home from home for us – even if people find our accents strange, we still think of ourselves as an Irish family. Grandad says we're not the only ones – about 10% of people living in Britain have Irish ancestors. That's about six million people – let's hope they're all cheering us on in October!

Think About It

1. During the early 1950s there was plenty of work available in construction and nursing in the United Kingdom. Why do you think this was?

2. Rural counties of Ireland suffered the most from loss of people to emigration. Why do you think this was? How do you think this affected the people left behind?

Did You Know?

During the 1950s in Ireland electricity was brought to most of the country. Households began to benefit from running water and indoor bathrooms in this decade. Television sets, however, were still rare and there was no Irish television channel until 1961.

The Key to Literacy

1950s emigrants from Ireland were often unsure when they would see their families again. The cost of travel was higher in those days, and without the internet, it was not that easy to stay in contact. They left the country with mixed feelings of sorrow, hope, betrayal and regret.

Imagine you are a child whose family is emigrating to America in the 1950s. Write a diary entry describing the journey, and your thoughts about your future life in America.

Remember:

- You are leaving behind your home, your friends, your grandparents.
- You might never see your village again.
- You are going to start a new life in America!

The 1980s – A New Wave of Emigration

In the 1980s, due to a combination of government overspending in the late 1970s, and a global downturn, the Irish economy suffered and unemployment figures rose. A new wave of emigration from Ireland began. This became known as the 'Brain Drain' because many of the people who left the country were bright and talented young graduates. In the early 1980s, 8% of university graduates left the country to find work. By the end of the 1980s, this had risen to 30%.

Unemployment in Ireland reached 18% by the late 1980s. Those who left Ireland in the 1980s went to thriving countries like the UK, America, Australia, New Zealand and Canada where the standard of living was much better. Many became citizens of their new countries, married and had children. The children of Irish emigrants are called 'second-generation' Irish.

Checkpoint

1. What was the 'Brain Drain'?

2. What was the unemployment rate in the late 1980s?

3. Where did the Irish emigrate to in the 1980s?

Design and Draw

In 1986 Irish musicians organised a rock concert in Dublin to highlight the crisis of Ireland's unemployment problem. This concert was called Self Aid. They used the slogan 'Make it Work'. Imagine a similar concert is being held in your locality to raise awareness of a local or national crisis. Think of a name for the concert. Design a poster advertising the event. Think of a good slogan for your poster. What kind of imagery would you use?

Over to You

Interview a person who has lived through the 1980s. Ask them what they remember from the decade and to compare the 1980s with the present day. What things were similar? What things were different? Use a recording device to record the interview, and then write down the interview in a question and answer format.

The 1990s Onwards – Immigration and Emigration

In the middle of the 1990s Ireland entered a new phase of prosperity. Jobs were created when large US companies began to locate in Ireland. Ireland offered an educated workforce, access to EU markets, and a low taxation rate for businesses. Many of these companies were fast-growing technology and pharmaceutical companies. Unemployment figures in Ireland dropped to 4.5% and the numbers of people emigrating reduced. This period of history was called the Celtic Tiger. It lasted from the mid 1990s to 2007.

During the Celtic Tiger years there was an increase in the number of immigrant workers arriving in Ireland. Thousands of people came to Ireland from Poland and other eastern European countries, and from African countries such as Nigeria. Immigrants arriving in Ireland were looking for work and a better life for their families. Some of these people sent the money they earned in Ireland back to their families at home.

The Celtic Tiger ended in 2007. A year later Ireland went into a recession. This means that there was a decline in the economy and wealth of Ireland. Many other countries also experienced a recession. Emigration returned as a part of daily life. In 2011, an estimated 60,000 people left our shores for the UK, Canada, the USA, Australia and New Zealand. With today's internet technologies, it is easier for Irish emigrants to stay connected to family and friends back home than it was in previous generations.

Fact File

In 2011, immigrants made up over 10% of Ireland's population. Eastern European, African and Asian people, as well as a large number of people from the UK, made up this percentage. Census records show that there were 122,585 Poles living in Ireland in 2011.

Did You Know?

There are 70 million people around the world who claim to be Irish or Irish descendants. 41 million of these people live in the USA.

The New Faces of Ireland

Blog

My name is Danuwa and I am a 5th class pupil in Portlaoise, County Laois. I was born in Nigeria, a large country in Africa, but my parents moved here when I was just two years old. My father works as an engineer, and my mother is a beautician.

Even though we are African immigrants living in Ireland I like to think of myself as Irish now. I don't remember my life in Nigeria, or who my friends were before we lived in Ireland. My parents say that our life here is better than it was in Nigeria. When people meet me first I think they are surprised to hear my Irish accent! They sometimes have a problem pronouncing my name – but I don't mind. We have started to learn Irish as a family – we go to classes in the evening at the local library. We were very proud to be living here when a Nigerian man was elected mayor of Portlaoise – my parents say that was a great day for Irish-Nigerian integration. Every year I take part in the St Patrick's Day parade – that's my way of letting people know I value the heritage of my new country!

History Detective

The Irish Polish Society was formed in 1979 in Ireland by a group of Polish people and Irish supporters. During the early 1980s, Poland was a country in crisis and the Society organised sending aid to Poland by holding fundraising events. Research the full history of the Irish Polish Society. Why was Poland in crisis in the 1980s? What type of aid did the Society organise? What kind of work and events does the Society organise today?

Date It!

Find out when decimal currency was introduced to Ireland.
Then find out when the euro currency was introduced to Ireland.

Lesson Wrap-Up

Visual Summary

Unemployment caused mass emigration from Ireland during the 1950s. Over 400,000 people left Ireland, many going to the UK.

In the 1960s new government policies created jobs for Irish people. People no longer had to emigrate to find work. Emigration returned in the 1980s.

During the Celtic Tiger years, immigrants began to arrive in Ireland. However, after 2007, when the Celtic Tiger ended, emigration returned.

What Did I Learn?

What have I learned in this chapter?

_____

_____

What else would I like to know?

_____

_____

Where can I find this information?

_____

_____

Review

1. **Recall**

   What was the unemployment rate during the Celtic Tiger years?

2. **Vocabulary**

   Draw a picture that shows the difference between emigration and immigration.

3. **Critical Thinking**

   Immigration has changed Irish society. Many people of different nationalities now call Ireland home. How has this affected Irish society in a positive way? Are there any negative effects?

4. **Be a Historian!**

   Make a timeline showing events in Ireland from the 1950s to the present day. Use information from this chapter, from interviewing people and other sources such as the internet and books to help you.

Glossary

A

alliances

friendly connections or associations between countries.

allies

people or countries that cooperate with or help one another in a particular activity, e.g. in a war.

Áras an Uachtaráin

the home of the President of Ireland, located in the Phoenix Park in Dublin.

archaeologist

a person whose job it is to study ancient things.

Armed Forces

the military forces of a country including the army, navy, etc.

Armistice Day

the anniversary of the armistice of November 11, 1918.

assassinated

murdered in a surprise attack for political or religious reasons.

axles

the rods through the centre of a spinning wheel, on which it rotates.

Aztecs

the people who established an empire in Mexico before the Spanish conquest of 1521.

B

banshee

a female spirit whose wailing warns of an impending death in a house.

blight

a plant disease caused by fungi.

C

campaign

a planned series of actions, especially to arouse interest in something.

cargo

goods carried in a ship or by aircraft.

census

an official count or survey of the population.

charcoal

a black solid obtained when wood, bone or other organic matter is heated in the absence of air.

charity

giving money, help, etc. to other people.

civilians

people of a country who are not part of the armed forces.

codex

an ancient manuscript text in book form.

colonies

countries or areas under the control of another country.

comrades

friends or companions.

conquistadors

Spanish soldiers, adventurers and explorers who brought much of central and south America under Spanish control in the sixteenth century.

conscription

compulsory enlistment for state service, typically into the armed forces.

court martial

a military court to try persons for serious breaches of military law.

cravat

a short, wide strip of fabric worn by men around the neck and tucked inside an open-necked shirt.

D

denominational

relating to or according to the principles of a particular religious group.

downturn

a decline in economic, business, or other activity.

dullahan

a headless horseman from Irish mythology.

dunces

people of slow learning, especially in school.

dynasty

a succession of people from the same family who rule a country.

E

economic

relating to economics – the financial affairs of countries and the production and consumption of goods and services.

Egyptologist

a person whose job it is to study ancient Egypt.

emblem

an object that is symbolic of something.

emigrants

people who leaves their native country or region to settle in another.

emigration

the act of leaving one's native country or region to settle in another.

emperor

a man who rules an empire.

enclosure

an area that is sealed off with a barrier.

enlisted

to be enrolled in the armed services.

evicted

to be forced to move out of a house.

excavation

the act of uncovering something by digging.

excavate

uncovering something by digging.

F

famine

a severe shortage of food that can result in widespread starvation.

fieldwork

practical work conducted in the natural environment.

G

Good Friday Agreement

an agreement that promoted partnership, equality and respect between communities in Northern Ireland.

Gorgon

a terrifying female creature from Greek mythology.

graduate

someone who has been to a university or college and been awarded a degree

Great Wall of China

a fortified wall in Northern China built to protect the Chinese empire against invaders.

griddle

a metal plate hung over an open fire, used for cooking food.

heretic

a person holding opinions or beliefs at odds with what is generally accepted

hieroglyphics

writing in the form of hieroglyphs (small symbols).

home rule

self-government in local matters by a country that is ruled by another.

immigration

the act of coming to a new country and living there.

Irish Citizen Army

a group of trained volunteers established in Dublin to protect worker demonstrations against the police.

Irish Volunteers

a military organisation founded to protect the rights of the people of Ireland.

irrigation

the act of supplying land with water so that crops can grow.

lament

to express grief about something.

loyalists

supporters of the union between Great Britain and Northern Ireland.

magnetometer

an instrument used for measuring magnetic forces.

maize

a tall kind of corn with large seeds.

mandatory

required by rules or laws.

Medusa

a woman transformed into a gorgon by Athenain in Greek mythology.

Military

the armed forces of a country.

mission statement

a formal summary of the aims and values of a school, company, etc.

Mongol

a native or national of Mongolia.

Mortal

that can die, relating to human beings.

Mountjoy Prison

a prison located on the north side of Dublin.

P

paramilitary

an unofficial military force.

partition

the act of dividing a state or country into parts.

peace process

the discussions between the British and Irish governments, which aim to resolve the conflict in Northern Ireland.

periscope

a device using mirrors to let you see something on a higher level than where you are.

petticoat

a piece of women's clothing worn under a skirt or dress.

pharaoh

a ruler of ancient Egypt.

phoenix

a unique bird from mythology which was able to live for 500 years, then burn itself and rise from the ashes.

plantation

an early method of colonisation.

population

the total number of people who live in a particular area.

post holes

holes dug in the ground to hold a fence post.

power-sharing

a form of government in divided societies to prevent one group from dominating others; used in Northern Ireland.

prosperity

an economic state of growth with rising profits and full employment.

provinces

different parts of a country.

R

radiocarbon dating

a process that provides dates of objects by counting the radioactive decay of carbon in the remains of once living plants and animals.

recession

a period of temporary economic decline during which trade and industrial activity are reduced.

re-enact

to act out again.

refugees

people who have been forced to leave their country in order to escape war, persecution or natural disaster.

republicans

people who support the idea that Ireland should be an independent republic.

rising

an armed protest against authority.

Romanesque

a style of architecture that prevailed in Europe from AD 900 to AD 1200.

S

sacrifice

giving or doing something that you think will please a god, usually at your expense, or the expense of someone else.

Seanad Éireann

the upper house of the parliament of the Irish Republic.

segregation

the act of separating people of different races, religions, etc.

senator

a member of the senate, the upper house of parliament.

separatist

a person who supports the separation of a particular group of people from a larger body on the basis of ethnicity, religion or gender.

solstice

either of two times of the year when the sun is at its greatest distance from the equator, the summer solstice is the longest day of the year and the winter solstice is the shortest.

starvation

suffering or death caused by hunger.

structure

something that has been built or put together.

tenants

people who occupy land or property rented from a landlord.

terracotta

a hard red-brown unglazed earthenware, used for pottery and building construction.

treaty

a formally concluded and ratified agreement between countries.

Tutankhamun

a famous Egyptian pharaoh who began ruling Egypt as a young boy.

unemployment

the state of being without a job.

unionists

people in Northern Ireland, in particular a member of a political party, supporting or advocating union with Great Britain.

victory

success in a battle or war.

War of Independence

a war fought between 1919 and 1921 by the Irish Republican Army against the British government and its forces in Ireland.

workhouse

a place where the destitute of an area received food and lodging in return for work.

Zionist

a person holding the belief that there should be a Jewish national homeland in the historic land of Israel.